Tone's®
QUALITY SINCE 1873

Tone's
125th ANNIVERSARY
QUALITY SINCE 1873

easy entertaining

Tone's packaging has seen many innovations through their 125-year history. It has evolved from early paperboard and tin containers to glass and airtight clear plastic containers shown on pages 1–5.

set the tone
for terrific taste!

For 125 years, Tone's has shaped our nation's menu—with savory spices, tempting herbs and delightful flavorings that turn ordinary food into extraordinary cuisine. In this commemorative year, Tone's is pleased to present this keepsake collection of specially seasoned favorites.

Try any of the outstanding suggestions here, and you'll soon appreciate the value of using quality spices in making foods your friends and family will love. From Fresh Tomato Cheese Tart to no-bake Spiced Sugarplums, you'll discover new flavors for every occasion—casual or fancy, snack or feast. A dash here or a sprinkle there makes a world of difference in every creation!

Whether you're a serious cook or are feeding a busy, on-the-run family, you'll find these recipes appeal to your sense of good taste—and use easy-to-find ingredients.

Just turn the page and add spice to your life as you join with Tone's in a festive celebration!

Pictured on cover: Dijon-Glazed Chicken with Peppers (recipe, page 33)

table of contents

© Copyright, 1998 Tone Brothers, Inc.
All rights reserved. Printed in the U.S.A.
Produced by Meredith Integrated Marketing,
1716 Locust Street, Des Moines, Iowa 50309-3023.
Tone's®, Durkee®, DecACake®, Spice Islands®
and Spice Advice® are registered trademarks of
Tone Brothers, Inc. Fleischmann's® is a registered trademark of Nabisco, Inc., licensed to Burns Philp Food, Inc.
Library of Congress Catalog Card Number: 98-67488   ISBN 0-696-20950-0. Printing Number and Year: 5 4 3 21   01 00 99 98

Share in the

Tone's Tradition

Variety is the spice of life. And for more than 125 years, Tone's has supplied the many spices and flavorings that help create America's meals. Starting with the vision of one dedicated family, Tone's has built a legacy of quality and innovation that touches us all—even when we are unaware of the source.

Not content to serve consumers only through supermarkets with such leading national brands as Tone's®, Durkee®, Spice Islands® and DecACake®, Tone's supplies many restaurants, schools and other commercial food outlets with its quality products. It also was a pioneer supplier to wholesale clubs.

Because Tone's understands the importance of selecting just the right spices and flavorings for foods, it has built a long-standing tradition of consistently offering consumers new options and flavorful ideas for enhancing their eating pleasure. This book is designed to help Tone's customers spice up their lives with distinctive foods.

Jehiel and I.E. Tone, founding brothers of Tone Brothers, Inc.

Company Driven by Quality

Tone Brothers, Inc., was founded in 1873, when Jehiel Tone convinced his brother, Isaac E. Tone, to help him market coffee and spices. They decided to base the business in Des Moines, Iowa, which offered a central location and a wide-open opportunity to service the Midwest.

By 1884, Tone's product line consisted of seven spices: black pepper, cinnamon, nutmeg, cloves, allspice, mace and ginger. Tone's also became the first company west of the Mississippi to pack and sell ready-roasted coffee.

Throughout their history Tone's has been a pioneer in industry changes that provided consumers with high-quality products. For example, in 1888, Tone's introduced the revolutionary idea of selling pure ground pepper, as opposed to a heavier, less expensive "P.D. pepper," which was a blend of ground olive

stones, cayenne pepper and black coloring. Despite grocers' resistance, Tone's packaged the pepper (and, later, pure cinnamon) in individual consumer units.

Today, Tone's continues its quest for quality by sourcing spices and herbs from around the world. For example, they use a combination of Chinese and Cochin (India) ginger for the best flavor profile in its Spice Islands brand.

that the founding spirit of this innovative company lives on today. Tone's stands proud as a symbol of success and a reflection of our passion for great food.

This book is our way of sharing that passion. We know that you'll feel confident that you are serving the very best when you season foods with Tone's spices and flavorings. You'll also create savory memories for you and your family or friends. Enjoy!

Inspiring Innovations

 In 1897, Isaac's son, Jay E. Tone, Sr., came from the Massachusetts Institute of Technology in Boston to help the company build a new laboratory. Drawing on his chemical engineering degree, Jay patented an extract percolator that was used to develop vanilla, lemon and other fruit extracts that soon were added to Tone's growing product line. His invention still is used widely today.

The subsequent years brought continued advancements. Tone's eventually replaced paperboard and tin containers with airtight plastic packaging. Tone's was the first spice company to use clear plastic packaging to keep out air and moisture. And in 1982, with the help of Iowa State University research, Tone's developed a unique cryogenic grinding system to ensure superior quality and freshness of their spices.

Anniversary Celebration

As the company celebrates its 125th anniversary in 1998, Tone's boasts more than 2,000 varieties of seasonings and mixes. It's easy to see

all-occasion appetizers
plus snacks and beverages, too!

When you're looking for an impressive prelude, dip into High-Spirited Guacamole, grab a handful of Chili Spiced Nuts or sip on soothing Swedish Spiced Wine. Thanks to Tone's, these party pleasers will get your gathering off to a warm start!

Holiday Smoked Salmon Dip
(see recipe, page 10)

fresh tomato cheese tart

Makes 12 appetizer servings **PREP TIME: 10 minutes** **BAKE TIME: 50 minutes**

Prepared pie dough for one 9-inch pie shell

Filling
- ³⁄₄ cup ricotta cheese
- 1 egg
- ¹⁄₄ cup shredded mozzarella cheese
- ¹⁄₄ cup grated Parmesan cheese
- 1 teaspoon TONE'S Basil (leaves)
- ¹⁄₄ teaspoon TONE'S Ground Black Pepper
- ¹⁄₄ teaspoon TONE'S Thyme (leaves)
- ¹⁄₈ teaspoon TONE'S Rosemary (leaves), crushed

Topping
- 2 medium plum tomatoes, thinly sliced
- ¹⁄₂ teaspoon TONE'S Basil (leaves)
- ¹⁄₈ teaspoon TONE'S Rosemary (leaves), crushed
- 1 tablespoon olive oil

Place pie dough flat on ungreased baking sheet; generously pierce dough with fork. Bake the pie dough at 350°F for 20 minutes or until light brown.

In large bowl, combine filling ingredients; mix well. Spread on baked crust, leaving ¹⁄₄-inch border. Arrange tomatoes in circular pattern on filling. Sprinkle with ¹⁄₂ teaspoon basil and ¹⁄₈ teaspoon rosemary; drizzle with oil. Bake at 350°F for 30 minutes or until golden and bubbly. Cool slightly on wire rack; serve warm.

Nutrition information per serving (¹⁄₁₂ of recipe): calories 109; total fat 7 g; saturated fat 3 g; cholesterol 25 mg; sodium 140 mg; total carbohydrate 7 g; dietary fiber 0 g; protein 4 g

RECIPE NOTE: For convenience, use prepared pie dough from the refrigerator section of the supermarket.

visit our web site or call toll free
Throughout the book, look for this symbol for a number of helpful spice tips. For more great spice tips, visit www.spiceadvice.com on the Worldwide Web. Or, phone Spice Advice toll free at 1-800-247-5251.

pull-apart appetizer ring

Makes 1 ring
PREP TIME: 25 minutes   **PROOF TIME/REFRIGERATED: 2 to 24 hours**   **BAKE TIME: 35 minutes**

3^1/$_2$ to 4 cups all-purpose flour
  3 tablespoons sugar
  2 packages (4^1/$_2$ teaspoons) FLEISCHMANN'S Active Dry or RapidRise Yeast
1^1/$_2$ teaspoons TONE'S Italian Seasoning
  1 teaspoon salt
^{3}/$_4$ cup warm milk (105 to 115°F)

^{1}/$_4$ cup (^{1}/$_2$ stick) butter or margarine, softened
^{1}/$_4$ cup warm water (105 to 115°F)
  1 egg
  3 tablespoons butter or margarine, melted
  3 tablespoons Seed and Pepper Mix (see recipe, below) or poppy seed, divided

In large bowl, combine 1^1/$_2$ cups flour, sugar, undissolved yeast, Italian seasoning and salt. Gradually add milk, ^{1}/$_4$ cup butter and water to dry ingredients; beat 2 minutes at medium speed of electric mixer, scraping bowl occasionally. Add egg and ^{1}/$_2$ cup flour; beat 2 minutes at high speed, scraping bowl occasionally. With spoon, stir in enough remaining flour to make soft dough. Knead on floured surface until smooth and elastic, about 6 to 8 minutes. Cover; let rest 10 minutes.

Grease 10-inch tube pan with 1 tablespoon of the melted butter. (If pan has removable bottom, line with aluminum foil before buttering.) Sprinkle 1 tablespoon Seed and Pepper Mix in bottom of pan.

Divide dough into 30 equal pieces. Roll each into ball. Dip 15 balls in melted butter; place in pan. Sprinkle with 1 tablespoon Seed and Pepper Mix. Dip remaining balls in butter; place in pan, making second layer. Sprinkle with remaining Seed and Pepper Mix. Cover tightly with plastic wrap; refrigerate 2 to 24 hours.*

Remove from refrigerator. Uncover and let stand 10 minutes at room temperature. Bake at 375°F for 35 minutes or until done, covering with aluminum foil during last 15 minutes to prevent overbrowning, if necessary. Cool in pan on wire rack 20 minutes. Invert and unmold onto plate; serve warm.

SEED AND PEPPER MIX: In bowl, combine 1 teaspoon TONE'S Ground Black Pepper and enough poppy seed, sesame seed, whole caraway seed, whole celery seed and/or whole cumin seed to make 3 tablespoons.

Nutrition information per serving (^{1}/$_{30}$ **of recipe):** calories 97; total fat 3 g; saturated fat 2 g; cholesterol 15 mg; sodium 111 mg; total carbohydrate 14 g; dietary fiber 1 g; protein 2 g

*RECIPE NOTE: To bake immediately: Cover; let rise in warm, draft-free place until doubled in size, about 30 minutes. Bake as directed.

high-spirited guacamole

Makes 2½ cups   **PREP TIME: 10 minutes**   **STAND TIME: 15 minutes**

- 2 large ripe avocados, pitted, peeled
- ½ cup diced tomato
- 3 tablespoons fresh lime juice
- 1 tablespoon tequila, if desired

- 1 to 2 teaspoons TONE'S Crushed Red Pepper
- 1 teaspoon TONE'S Ground Cumin Seed
- ½ teaspoon salt
- ¼ teaspoon TONE'S Garlic Powder or 1½ teaspoons finely chopped garlic

In medium bowl, mash avocados coarsely with a fork. Stir in remaining ingredients; let stand 15 minutes to blend flavors. Garnish with lime wedges, if desired.

Nutrition information per serving (¼ cup): calories 71; total fat 6 g; saturated fat 1 g; cholesterol 0 mg; sodium 112 mg; total carbohydrate 4 g; dietary fiber 2 g; protein 1 g

RECIPE NOTE: *Serve guacamole as a dip for chips and raw vegetables; a topping for tacos, fajitas, burritos, burgers and salads; or an accompaniment to grilled meat and poultry.*

holiday smoked salmon dip

Makes 2 cups   **PREP TIME: 10 minutes**

- 1 cup light dairy sour cream
- 1 cup reduced-fat mayonnaise
- 2 ounces smoked salmon, cut into strips

- 1 teaspoon SPICE ISLANDS Beau Monde Seasoning
- ½ teaspoon TONE'S Dill Weed

In blender or food processor container, place all ingredients. Pulse on and off until blended and salmon is coarsely chopped. Cover and refrigerate several hours or overnight.

Nutrition information per serving (2 tablespoons): calories 74; total fat 6 g; saturated fat 2 g; cholesterol 3 mg; sodium 255 mg; total carbohydrate 3 g; dietary fiber 0 g; protein 2 g

RECIPE NOTE: *Serve dip with assorted cut-up vegetables, crackers or chips.*

Pictured on pages 6–7

High-Spirited Guacamole

greek cauliflower dip

Makes 3 cups **PREP TIME: 15 minutes** **COOK TIME: 10 to 20 minutes**

3 cups small cauliflower florets
(approximately 1 head)
1/3 cup crumbled feta cheese
2 tablespoons fresh lemon juice
1 teaspoon TONE'S Oregano (leaves)
1/2 teaspoon TONE'S Basil (leaves)
1/2 teaspoon TONE'S Garlic Powder
1/4 teaspoon salt
1/4 teaspoon TONE'S Ground Black Pepper
1/2 to 3/4 cup ready-to-serve chicken broth
2 tablespoons coarsely chopped pitted
kalamata olives

Cook cauliflower, as desired, until tender. In food processor container, combine cauliflower, cheese, lemon juice, oregano, basil, garlic powder, salt and pepper; process until finely chopped. Gradually add broth, processing until smooth and of desired consistency. Add olives; pulse just until olives are mixed in.

Nutrition information per serving (2 tablespoons): calories 12; total fat 1 g; saturated fat 0 g; cholesterol 2 mg; sodium 88 mg; total carbohydrate 1 g; dietary fiber 0 g; protein 1 g

RECIPE NOTES: To cook cauliflower, place in microwave-safe dish with 2 tablespoons water; cover and microwave on HIGH (100%) 7 to 9 minutes or until tender, stirring once. (Microwave ovens vary; cooking times may need to be adjusted.)

Serve dip with assorted colored bell pepper pieces, cucumber slices and pita bread wedges. Garnish with whole kalamata olives, as desired.

chili popcorn

Makes 3 quarts   **PREP TIME: 10 minutes**

2 teaspoons TONE'S Chili Powder	12 cups freshly popped popcorn
1/2 teaspoon TONE'S Garlic Salt	(1/2 cup unpopped)
1/4 teaspoon TONE'S Oregano (leaves)	3 tablespoons butter or margarine, melted

In small bowl, combine chili powder, garlic salt and oregano. Place popped popcorn in large plastic or paper bag; sprinkle with seasoning mixture. Close bag and shake to evenly distribute seasoning.

Drizzle butter over popcorn. Immediately close bag and shake until popcorn is evenly coated. Serve at once.

Nutrition information per serving (1 1/2 cups): calories 86; total fat 5 g; saturated fat 3 g; cholesterol 12 mg; sodium 84 mg; total carbohydrate 10 g; dietary fiber 2 g; protein 2 g

chili spiced nuts

Makes 2 cups   **PREP TIME: 5 minutes**   **COOK TIME: 7 to 9 minutes**

- 2 teaspoons olive or vegetable oil
- 1/4 teaspoon TONE'S Garlic Powder
- 1/4 teaspoon TONE'S Ground Cayenne Pepper
- 2 cups (12 ounces) salted peanuts, cashews, almonds or a combination
- 1/2 teaspoon TONE'S Chili Powder

In medium skillet, combine oil, garlic powder and cayenne pepper; heat mixture over medium heat until hot, stirring occasionally. Add nuts; cook and stir over medium heat 6 to 8 minutes or until nuts are toasted. Remove from heat; stir in chili powder. Serve warm or at room temperature.

Nutrition information per serving (3 tablespoons): calories 180; total fat 15 g; saturated fat 2 g; cholesterol 0 mg; sodium 239 mg; total carbohydrate 6 g; dietary fiber 2 g; protein 7 g

Swedish Spiced Wine

swedish spiced wine

Makes 16 servings   **PREP TIME: 5 minutes**   **COOK TIME: 8 minutes**

- 1 bottle (1.5 liters) dry red wine
- ½ cup sugar
- 3 TONE'S Cinnamon Sticks
- 1 tablespoon whole cloves
- 2 teaspoons freshly grated orange peel
- ½ cup raisins
- ⅓ cup whole blanched almonds
- 1 small orange, thinly sliced and halved

In large saucepan, combine wine, sugar, cinnamon sticks, cloves and orange peel. Heat over medium heat to simmering; barely simmer 5 minutes. (Do not boil.) Strain wine; return to pan. Add raisins and almonds; heat until just hot. Transfer to heatproof serving container; float orange slices on top.

Nutrition information per serving (approximately ½ cup): calories 126; total fat 2 g; saturated fat 0 g; cholesterol 0 mg; sodium 6 mg; total carbohydrate 13 g; dietary fiber 1 g; protein 1 g

VARIATION: For alcohol-free punch, substitute 1 bottle (64 ounces) cranberry juice cocktail for the wine; decrease sugar to ¼ cup.

Nutrition information per serving (approximately ½ cup): calories 118; total fat 2 g; saturated fat 0 g; cholesterol 0 mg; sodium 3 mg; total carbohydrate 26 g; dietary fiber 1 g; protein 1 g

saucy bloody mary mix

Makes 2 servings   **PREP TIME: 5 minutes**

- 1 can (11½ ounces) tomato juice
  or vegetable juice cocktail
- 2 tablespoons fresh lemon juice
- 2 teaspoons Worcestershire sauce
- ½ teaspoon TONE'S Celery Salt
  Ice cubes
  Lemon slices or celery tops (optional)

In pitcher, combine tomato juice, lemon juice, Worcestershire sauce and celery salt; mix well. Pour over ice in glasses; garnish with lemon slices or celery tops, if desired. (For Bloody Mary, add 3 fluid ounces vodka per glass.)

Nutrition information per serving without vodka (approximately 1 cup): calories 43; total fat 0 g; saturated fat 0 g; cholesterol 0 mg; sodium 801 mg; total carbohydrate 10 g; dietary fiber 1 g; protein 2 g

mouthwatering main dishes
from near and far

For something deliciously different, these seasoned sensations are a taste adventure—and equally exciting to prepare with Tone's herbs and spices! Incorporating flavors from around the world, you'll find fresh ideas for your holiday table, as well as classic home-style favorites.

Sherried Beef Stir-Fry (see recipe, page 18)

sherried beef stir-fry

Makes 4 servings
PREP TIME: 15 minutes   **MARINATE TIME: 15 to 30 minutes**   **COOK TIME: 8 to 10 minutes**

3/4   pound well-trimmed boneless beef
       top sirloin steak, cut into thin strips
2   tablespoons peanut or vegetable oil, divided
6   cups sliced bok choy or Swiss chard
       (1 medium head)
1   large red bell pepper, cut into thin strips
2   teaspoons sesame seed, toasted
       (see tip, page 37)

Marinade
1/2   cup dry sherry
3   tablespoons packed brown sugar
3   tablespoons soy sauce
1   tablespoon TONE'S Cornstarch
1   teaspoon ground ginger
3/4   teaspoon TONE'S Garlic Powder
       or 1 tablespoon finely chopped garlic
1/4   teaspoon TONE'S Ground Black Pepper

In medium bowl, combine marinade ingredients; add beef, tossing to coat. Cover and marinate in refrigerator 15 to 30 minutes. With slotted spoon, remove beef from marinade; reserve marinade. In large skillet or wok, heat 1 tablespoon oil over medium-high heat until hot; stir-fry beef, 1/2 at a time, 1 to 2 minutes or until outside surface is browned. (Do not overcook.) Remove from pan.

In same pan, stir-fry bok choy and bell pepper in remaining 1 tablespoon oil 1 to 2 minutes or until crisp-tender. Stir in reserved marinade; bring to a boil. Cook 1 minute or until sauce is thickened, stirring occasionally. Return beef to pan; toss. If desired, serve with hot cooked rice and sprinkle with toasted sesame seed.

Nutrition information per serving (1/4 of recipe): calories 284; total fat 12 g; saturated fat 3 g; cholesterol 56 mg; sodium 418 mg; total carbohydrate 17 g; dietary fiber 2 g; protein 22 g

Pictured on pages 16–17

beef tenderloin
with horseradish cream sauce

Makes 8 to 10 servings   **PREP TIME: 10 minutes**   **ROAST TIME: 50 to 60 minutes**

1   (4-pound) whole beef tenderloin roast, well trimmed

Sauce
- ½ cup mayonnaise
- ½ cup sour cream
- 3 tablespoons prepared horseradish
- 1 tablespoon TONE'S Parsley Flakes

Seasoning
- 1 tablespoon SPICE ISLANDS Juniper Berries
- 1 tablespoon TONE'S Whole Black Pepper
- 2 teaspoons TONE'S Thyme (leaves)
- 1 teaspoon whole allspice

In small bowl, combine sauce ingredients; mix well. Cover and refrigerate 30 minutes or overnight.

In blender or mini food processor container, combine seasoning ingredients; process until fine. Press evenly onto surface of roast. Place roast on rack in shallow roasting pan. Insert ovenproof meat thermometer so tip is centered in thickest part of roast.

Roast at 425°F for 50 to 60 minutes for medium rare doneness. Remove roast when meat thermometer registers 135°F for medium rare. Transfer to carving board; tent loosely with aluminum foil and let stand 10 minutes. (Temperature will continue to rise 10°F to reach desired doneness and roast will be easier to carve.) Carve crosswise into slices. Serve with horseradish cream sauce.

Nutrition information per serving (⅛ **of recipe**): calories 499; total fat 31 g; saturated fat 10 g; cholesterol 155 mg; sodium 201 mg; total carbohydrate 3 g; dietary fiber 1 g; protein 49 g

informal supper buffet

For an easy buffet meal, prepare Beef Tenderloin with Horseradish Cream Sauce. Chill the roast beef and serve it sliced with small rolls or mini croissants and the horseradish sauce. Accompany the mini sandwiches with French Potato Salad (see recipe, page 55) and Mediterranean Orange and Kalamata Salad (see recipe, page 52). For dessert, prepare the Hazelnut Chiffon Cake with Mocha Buttercream (see recipe, page 84).

Hibachi Beef Kabobs

hibachi beef kabobs

Makes 4 servings
PREP TIME: 15 minutes   **MARINATE TIME: 2 hours or overnight**   **COOK TIME: 8 to 11 minutes**

1¼ pounds boneless beef top sirloin steak,
        cut 1 inch thick
2 small red or green bell peppers,
        cut into 1½-inch pieces
2 small crookneck squash,
        cut into ½-inch-thick slices
¼ pound mushrooms
2 teaspoons sesame seed

Marinade
¼ cup vegetable oil
¼ cup SPICE ISLANDS Rice Vinegar
2 tablespoons frozen orange juice
        concentrate, thawed
2 tablespoons soy sauce
1 teaspoon TONE'S Onion Powder
¾ teaspoon SPICE ISLANDS Chinese Five Spice
¾ teaspoon freshly ground
        TONE'S Whole Black Pepper

Trim fat from steak; cut into 1- to 1½-inch pieces. In plastic bag, combine marinade ingredients; add beef, turning to coat. Close bag securely and marinate in refrigerator 2 hours or overnight, turning occasionally.

Remove beef from marinade; reserve marinade. Alternately thread beef and vegetables onto four 12-inch metal skewers. Grill over medium coals 8 to 11 minutes for medium rare to medium doneness, turning and brushing occasionally with reserved marinade. (Do not brush during last 4 to 5 minutes of grilling.) Sprinkle with sesame seed before serving.

Nutrition information per serving (1 kabob): calories 342; total fat 19 g; saturated fat 4 g; cholesterol 93 mg; sodium 241 mg; total carbohydrate 9 g; dietary fiber 2 g; protein 34 g

RECIPE NOTE: To broil, place kabobs on rack in broiler pan so kabobs are 3 to 4 inches from heat. Broil 8 to 10 minutes for medium rare to medium doneness, turning and brushing occasionally with marinade. (Do not brush during last 4 to 5 minutes of broiling.)

peppered steak diane

Makes 6 servings   **PREP TIME: 10 minutes**   **COOK TIME: 15 to 20 minutes**

1½ pounds boneless beef top sirloin steak,
     cut 1 inch thick
1 tablespoon freshly ground
     TONE'S Whole Black Pepper
2 tablespoons vegetable oil
     TONE'S Garlic Salt

Sauce

¼ cup brandy or dry red wine
1 teaspoon Worcestershire sauce
2 tablespoons butter or margarine

Cut steak into serving-size pieces. Press pepper evenly onto both sides of steaks. In large skillet, heat oil over medium-high heat until hot; pan-fry steaks 12 to 18 minutes for medium rare to medium doneness, turning once. Remove from heat. Season steaks with garlic salt, as desired; transfer to warm platter.

For sauce, add brandy and Worcestershire sauce to skillet; bring to a boil. Cook and stir until browned bits attached to skillet are dissolved and liquid is reduced by ½; remove from heat. Whisk in butter; pour over steaks.

Nutrition information per serving (⅙ of recipe): calories 263; total fat 14 g; saturated fat 5 g; cholesterol 85 mg; sodium 153 mg; total carbohydrate 1 g; dietary fiber 0 g; protein 26 g

lemon pepper burgers

Makes 4 servings   **PREP TIME: 10 minutes**   **COOK TIME: 10 to 13 minutes**

1 pound lean ground beef or turkey
⅓ cup shredded sharp cheddar cheese
     or crumbled blue cheese
2 teaspoons Worcestershire sauce

2 teaspoons TONE'S Lemon Pepper, divided
½ teaspoon TONE'S Garlic Powder
     Hamburger buns, sliced tomato,
     lettuce (optional)

In medium bowl, combine ground beef, cheese, Worcestershire sauce, 1 teaspoon lemon pepper and garlic powder, mixing lightly but thoroughly. Shape into four ½-inch-thick patties. Press remaining lemon pepper evenly onto both sides of patties. Pan-fry, grill or broil patties 10 to 13 minutes or until no longer pink in center, turning once. Serve burgers in buns with tomato and lettuce, if desired.

Nutrition information per serving (1 burger): calories 255; total fat 16 g; saturated fat 7 g; cholesterol 81 mg; sodium 233 mg; total carbohydrate 2 g; dietary fiber 0 g; protein 24 g

burgundy steak strips

Makes 4 servings
PREP TIME: 12 minutes   **MARINATE TIME: 30 minutes**   **COOK TIME: 10 to 15 minutes**

- 1 pound well-trimmed boneless beef top sirloin steak, cut into thin strips
- 2 tablespoons all-purpose flour
- 2 tablespoons tomato paste
- 3/4 cup ready-to-serve beef broth
- 1/2 teaspoon TONE'S Ground Black Pepper
- 2 tablespoons vegetable oil, divided
- Salt

- 1/4 pound small whole mushrooms
- 1 small onion, sliced

Marinade
- 2/3 cup SPICE ISLANDS Burgundy Cooking Wine
- 1 teaspoon TONE'S Rosemary (leaves), crushed
- 1 teaspoon TONE'S Thyme (leaves)

In medium bowl, combine marinade ingredients; add beef, tossing to coat. Cover and marinate in refrigerator 30 minutes. With slotted spoon, remove beef from marinade; set aside. Whisk flour and tomato paste into marinade until smooth. Stir in broth and pepper; set aside.

In large skillet, heat 1 tablespoon oil over medium-high heat until hot; cook and stir beef, 1/2 at a time, 1 to 2 minutes or until outside surface is browned. (Do not overcook.) Remove from pan; season with salt, as desired.

In same pan, cook and stir mushrooms and onion in remaining 1 tablespoon oil 3 to 4 minutes or until crisp-tender. Stir in marinade; bring to a boil. Cook 1 minute or until sauce is thickened, stirring occasionally. Return beef to pan; toss.

Nutrition information per serving (1/4 of recipe): calories 288; total fat 14 g; saturated fat 3 g; cholesterol 75 mg; sodium 625 mg; total carbohydrate 8 g; dietary fiber 1 g; protein 28 g

Mesa Corn with Chili-Seasoned Pork

mesa corn
with chili-seasoned pork

Makes 4 servings　　　　　**PREP TIME: 25 minutes**　　　　**COOK TIME: 20 to 25 minutes**

2 tablespoons all-purpose flour	**Lime Sour Cream**
1½ teaspoons TONE'S Chili Powder	1 cup sour cream
½ teaspoon salt	1 tablespoon fresh lime juice
½ teaspoon TONE'S Ground Cayenne Pepper	1 teaspoon freshly grated lime peel
1 pound boneless pork loin chops, cut ½ to ¾ inch thick	
3 tablespoons vegetable oil, divided	
2 large red bell peppers, diced	
1 package (10 ounces) frozen whole kernel corn	

In small bowl, combine lime sour cream ingredients; set aside.

In shallow dish, combine flour, chili powder, salt and cayenne pepper. Pound pork to ¼-inch thickness; dredge in flour mixture to coat both sides. Set aside.

In large skillet, heat 1 tablespoon oil over medium-high heat until hot; cook and stir bell peppers 6 to 8 minutes or until tender and lightly browned. Stir in corn; cover and cook 2 minutes. Season with additional salt and cayenne pepper, if desired. Transfer to platter; keep warm.

In same skillet, heat 1 tablespoon oil over medium-high heat until hot; pan-fry ½ of the pork chops 3 to 5 minutes for medium doneness, turning once. Repeat with remaining 1 tablespoon oil and remaining pork chops. Arrange pork on corn mixture; drizzle with lime sour cream. If desired, sprinkle lightly with cayenne pepper and garnish with fresh cilantro and lime slices.

Nutrition information per serving (¼ of recipe): calories 471; total fat 32 g; saturated fat 12 g; cholesterol 84 mg; sodium 352 mg; total carbohydrate 23 g; dietary fiber 3 g; protein 25 g

pork chops
with fennel and rosemary

Makes 4 servings   **PREP TIME: 5 minutes**   **COOK TIME: 14 to 16 minutes**

4 teaspoons olive oil
4 pork loin chops (bone-in), cut 1 inch thick
Seasoning
2 teaspoons fennel seed
2 teaspoons TONE'S Garlic Powder

2 teaspoons TONE'S Rosemary (leaves)
1½ teaspoons TONE'S Onion Powder
¾ teaspoon salt
¾ teaspoon TONE'S Ground Black Pepper

In blender or mini food processor container, combine seasoning ingredients; process until fine. Stir in oil; spread evenly on both sides of pork chops. Grill over medium coals 14 to 16 minutes for medium doneness, turning once.

Nutrition information per serving (1 chop): calories 213; total fat 12 g; saturated fat 3 g; cholesterol 64 mg; sodium 488 mg; total carbohydrate 3 g; dietary fiber 0 g; protein 22 g

pasta pizzazz

Makes 4 servings   **PREP TIME: 15 minutes**   **COOK TIME: 25 minutes**

8 ounces uncooked spaghetti or vermicelli
1 pound mild Italian sausages
1 medium onion, chopped
1 medium green or red bell pepper,
    cut into thin strips

½ cup dry white wine or ready-to-serve
    chicken broth
1 teaspoon TONE'S Oregano (leaves)
½ teaspoon TONE'S Basil (leaves)
½ teaspoon TONE's Crushed Red Pepper

Cook pasta as package directs; drain and keep warm. Meanwhile in large skillet, brown sausages on all sides over medium-high heat; remove from pan. Cut into ½-inch-thick slices; return to pan. Add onion and bell pepper; cook and stir 5 minutes. Stir in wine, oregano, basil and crushed red pepper; bring to a boil. Reduce heat; simmer 10 minutes. Serve sausage mixture over hot pasta.

Nutrition information per serving (¼ of recipe): calories 447; total fat 16 g; saturated fat 5 g; cholesterol 45 mg; sodium 338 mg; total carbohydrate 50 g; dietary fiber 3 g; protein 20 g

coconut pork stir-fry

Makes 4 to 6 servings
PREP TIME: 20 minutes   **MARINATE TIME: 15 minutes**   **COOK TIME: 20 minutes**

³/₄ pound pork tenderloin, cut lengthwise
    in half, then crosswise into
    ¹/₄-inch-thick slices
1 tablespoon vegetable oil
¹/₂ pound mushrooms, cut into
    ¹/₄-inch-thick slices
1 red bell pepper, cut into thin slices
1 small onion, cut into thin wedges
1 can (13¹/₂ ounces) coconut milk
1 teaspoon TONE'S Garlic Salt
4 cups packed spinach leaves
    (approximately 5 ounces)

Marinade
1 tablespoon soy sauce
1 teaspoon ground ginger
¹/₂ teaspoon SPICE ISLANDS Chinese Five Spice
¹/₂ teaspoon TONE'S Crushed Red Pepper

In medium bowl, combine marinade ingredients; add pork, tossing to coat. Cover and marinate in refrigerator 15 minutes. In large skillet or wok, heat oil over medium-high heat until hot; stir-fry pork, ¹/₂ at a time, 1 to 2 minutes or until outside surface is browned. With slotted spoon, remove pork from pan.

In same pan, stir-fry mushrooms, bell pepper and onion 3 to 5 minutes or until onion is crisp-tender. Add pork, coconut milk and garlic salt. Stir in spinach; cook 3 to 5 minutes or until spinach is wilted, stirring occasionally.

Nutrition information per serving (¹/₄ of recipe): calories 392; total fat 30 g; saturated fat 22 g; cholesterol 49 mg; sodium 483 mg; total carbohydrate 13 g; dietary fiber 5 g; protein 23 g

Baked Ham with Apricot Mustard Sauce

baked ham
with apricot mustard sauce

Makes 14 to 18 servings   **PREP TIME: 15 minutes**   **BAKE TIME: 1$^1/_2$ to 1$^3/_4$ hours**

1 (5- to 7-pound) fully-cooked bone-in ham or (4- to 5-pound) fully-cooked boneless ham
   Whole cloves
2 to 3 tablespoons water

Sauce
1 can (17 ounces) apricot halves, undrained
1 tablespoon Dijon-style mustard
1 teaspoon SPICE ISLANDS White Wine Vinegar
$^1/_8$ teaspoon TONE'S Ground Cinnamon

Glaze
$^1/_3$ cup apricot preserves
1 tablespoon Dijon-style mustard

In blender or food processor container, combine sauce ingredients; process 1 minute or until smooth. Set aside.

Score top of ham in diamond pattern; insert a whole clove in crossed point of each diamond. Place ham in shallow roasting pan; add water. Bake at 325°F as package directs (approximately 13 to 18 minutes per pound for bone-in ham; 19 to 23 minutes per pound for boneless ham).

In small bowl, combine glaze ingredients; brush over ham during last 20 minutes of baking time. Heat sauce until warm; serve with ham.

Nutrition information per serving ($^1/_{14}$ **of recipe**): calories 436; total fat 27 g; saturated fat 10 g; cholesterol 100 mg; sodium 1,982 mg; total carbohydrate 11 g; dietary fiber 0 g; protein 35g

spice advice: store them right

Keep spices and herbs in tightly covered containers in a cool, dry place away from heat, light and moisture that rob them of flavor. Some seeds high in oil, such as sesame seed, are best stored in the refrigerator or freezer to prevent them from becoming rancid. In general, whole spices and herbs stay fresh longer than ground spices and herbs.

mediterranean chicken

Makes 4 servings   **PREP TIME: 5 minutes**   **BAKE TIME: 20 to 25 minutes**

- 4 boneless chicken breast halves
- $^1/_4$ to $^1/_2$ teaspoon salt

Seasoning

- 2 tablespoons fresh lemon juice
- 2 tablespoons olive oil
- 1 teaspoon TONE'S Oregano (leaves)
- $^1/_8$ teaspoon TONE'S Garlic Powder or 1 clove garlic, finely chopped

In small bowl, combine seasoning ingredients. In baking pan, place chicken in single layer. Pour seasoning over chicken; turn to coat. Sprinkle with salt. Bake at 375°F for 20 to 25 minutes or until done.

Nutrition information per serving (1 chicken breast half): calories 257; total fat 14 g; saturated fat 3 g; cholesterol 82 mg; sodium 203 mg; total carbohydrate 1 g; dietary fiber 0 g; protein 29g

cajun chicken

Makes 4 servings   **PREP TIME: 5 minutes**   **COOK TIME: 10 to 15 minutes**

- 4 boneless skinless chicken breast halves

Seasoning

- $1^1/_2$ teaspoons TONE'S Thyme (leaves)
- 1 teaspoon TONE'S Garlic Salt
- 1 teaspoon TONE'S Onion Powder
- 1 teaspoon TONE'S Ground Cayenne Pepper
- $^3/_4$ teaspoon TONE'S Ground Black Pepper
- $^3/_4$ teaspoon TONE'S Ground White Pepper

In small bowl, combine seasoning ingredients; press evenly onto chicken. Sauté, grill or broil, as desired, until done.

Nutrition information per serving (1 chicken breast half): calories 169; total fat 5 g; saturated fat 1 g; cholesterol 73 mg; sodium 216 mg; total carbohydrate 2 g; dietary fiber 1 g; protein 27g

fajita chicken salad

Makes 4 servings   **PREP TIME: 15 minutes**   **COOK TIME: 10 minutes**

1 pound boneless skinless chicken breasts,
    cut into ¹/₂-inch-thick strips
¹/₄ cup vegetable oil
2 red or green bell peppers, sliced
1 red onion, sliced
¹/₄ cup SPICE ISLANDS Red Wine Vinegar
    (Garlic or regular flavor)
4 cups torn lettuce
2 tomatoes, sliced
1 avocado, pitted, peeled, sliced
    Warmed flour tortillas, prepared salsa
    and sour cream (optional)

Seasoning
1¹/₂ teaspoons TONE'S Ground Cumin Seed
1¹/₂ teaspoons TONE'S Oregano (leaves)
1 teaspoon salt
1 teaspoon TONE'S Garlic Powder
¹/₂ teaspoon TONE'S Spanish Paprika
¹/₂ teaspoon TONE'S Ground Cayenne
    Pepper

In medium bowl, combine seasoning ingredients; add chicken, tossing to coat. Set aside.

In large skillet, heat oil over medium-high heat until hot; cook and stir bell peppers and red onion 2 to 3 minutes or until crisp-tender. Add chicken; cook and stir 3 to 5 minutes or until center is no longer pink. Remove from heat; drizzle with vinegar and toss to coat.

Arrange lettuce, tomatoes and avocado on individual plates; top with chicken mixture. Serve with tortillas, salsa and sour cream, if desired.

Nutrition information per serving (¹/₄ of recipe): calories 378; total fat 25 g; saturated fat 4 g; cholesterol 63 mg; sodium 607 mg; total carbohydrate 14 g; dietary fiber 5 g; protein 26 g

spice advice: red spices

Check the color of red powdered spices, such as chili powder, cayenne and paprika. As they lose their freshness, these spices turn from red to brown in color and won't be as flavorful as when they were fresh. Store them in the refrigerator so they will hold their color and keep their flavor longer.

Dijon-Glazed Chicken with Peppers

dijon-glazed chicken
with peppers

Makes 4 servings   **PREP TIME: 15 minutes**   **COOK TIME: 15 to 20 minutes**

- 2 tablespoons olive oil
- 1½ pounds assorted red, green or yellow bell peppers, cut into thin strips
- 1 teaspoon TONE'S Garlic Salt
- ½ teaspoon freshly ground TONE'S Whole Black Pepper
- 4 boneless chicken breast halves

Glaze
- 2 tablespoons honey
- 2 tablespoons Dijon-style mustard
- 1 teaspoon SPICE ISLANDS White Wine Vinegar
- ½ teaspoon tarragon

In small bowl, combine glaze ingredients; set aside.

In large skillet, heat oil over medium-high heat until hot; cook and stir bell peppers 6 to 8 minutes or until tender. Season with garlic salt and pepper; keep warm.

Grill chicken over medium coals 9 to 11 minutes or until done, turning once and brushing occasionally with glaze. (Do not brush during last 3 to 4 minutes of grilling.) Serve with peppers.

Nutrition information per serving (¼ of recipe): calories 330; total fat 15 g; saturated fat 3 g; cholesterol 82 mg; sodium 367 mg; total carbohydrate 18 g; dietary fiber 3 g; protein 31 g

RECIPE NOTE: To broil, place chicken on rack in broiler pan so chicken is 3 to 4 inches from heat. Broil 15 to 18 minutes or until done, turning once and brushing occasionally with glaze. (Do not brush during last 7 to 9 minutes of broiling.)

Pictured on the cover

herbed burgers
with cucumber yogurt sauce

Makes 4 burgers   **PREP TIME: 10 minutes**   **COOK TIME: 10 to 12 minutes**

- 1 pound ground turkey
- 1/2 cup unseasoned dry bread crumbs
- 2 tablespoons milk
- 2 teaspoons TONE'S Lemon Pepper
- 1/2 teaspoon TONE'S Oregano (leaves)
- 4 whole pita breads, top 1/3 cut off, warmed
  Sliced tomato, sliced onion and crumbled feta cheese

Sauce
- 1 cup plain lowfat yogurt
- 2/3 cup finely chopped cucumber
- 1 teaspoon onion salt
- 1 teaspoon sugar

In small bowl, combine sauce ingredients; mix well. Set aside. In large bowl, combine turkey, bread crumbs, milk, lemon pepper and oregano, mixing lightly but thoroughly. Shape into four 1/2-inch-thick oval patties.

Grill patties over medium coals 10 to 14 minutes or until cooked through and juices run clear, turning once. Serve in pitas with sauce and tomato, onion and cheese, as desired.

Nutrition information per serving (1 burger): calories 451; total fat 16 g; saturated fat 6 g; cholesterol 73 mg; sodium 1,185 mg; total carbohydrate 43 g; dietary fiber 2 g; protein 31 g

RECIPE NOTE: To broil, place patties on rack in broiler pan so surface of meat is 3 to 4 inches from heat. Broil 10 to 12 minutes or until done, turning once.

quesadilla pie

Makes 4 servings   **PREP TIME: 20 minutes**   **COOK/BAKE TIME: 50 minutes**

1^1/$_2$ cups shredded cooked chicken
^{1}/$_4$ cup mild prepared salsa
1 tablespoon butter or margarine,
 softened, divided
3 large flour tortillas (10-inch diameter)
1 cup shredded cheddar cheese, divided
 TONE'S Chili Powder (optional)
 TONE'S Oregano (leaves) (optional)

Rice Mixture
3 tablespoons butter or margarine
^{3}/$_4$ cup uncooked long grain white rice
3 tablespoons TONE'S Dried Chopped Onion
1 tablespoon TONE'S Chicken Soup Base
1 teaspoon TONE'S Chili Powder
1 teaspoon TONE'S Oregano (leaves)
^{1}/$_8$ teaspoon TONE'S Garlic Powder
1^1/$_2$ cups water
1^1/$_2$ cups shredded cheddar cheese

Toppings
 Salsa, sliced avocado, sour cream (optional)

In small bowl, combine chicken and salsa; toss and set aside.

Prepare rice mixture. In medium saucepan, heat butter over medium heat until hot; cook and stir rice until golden. Stir in onion, soup base, chili powder, oregano and garlic powder. Add water; bring to a boil. Reduce heat; cover and simmer 20 minutes or until liquid is absorbed. Remove from heat; let stand, covered, 5 minutes. Stir in cheese; set aside.

Spread ^{1}/$_2$ tablespoon butter on one side of one tortilla; place, buttered side down, on baking sheet. Layer remaining ingredients as follows: rice mixture, second tortilla, ^{1}/$_2$ cup cheese, chicken mixture, remaining ^{1}/$_2$ cup cheese, remaining tortilla. Spread top tortilla with remaining ^{1}/$_2$ tablespoon butter. Sprinkle with chili powder and oregano, if desired.

Bake at 400°F for 20 minutes or until hot. Cut into 4 wedges. Top with salsa, avocado and sour cream, if desired.

Nutrition information per serving (^{1}/$_4$ of recipe): calories 779; total fat 41 g; saturated fat 24 g; cholesterol 152 mg; sodium 1,240 mg; total carbohydrate 60 g; dietary fiber 3 g; protein 41 g

Spicy-Sweet Chicken and Broccoli

spicy-sweet chicken
and broccoli

Makes 4 servings
PREP TIME: 15 minutes   **MARINATE TIME: 15 to 30 minutes**   **COOK TIME: 8 to 10 minutes**

1 pound boneless skinless chicken breasts, cut into $3/4$-inch pieces
2 tablespoons peanut or vegetable oil, divided
1 pound broccoli, cut into bite-size pieces
$1/2$ cup ready-to-serve chicken broth, divided
1 tablespoon TONE'S Cornstarch
2 tablespoons sesame seed, toasted

Marinade
$1/4$ cup packed brown sugar
3 tablespoons soy sauce
1 teaspoon ground ginger
$1/2$ to 1 teaspoon TONE'S Crushed Red Pepper

In medium bowl, combine marinade ingredients; add chicken, tossing to coat. Cover and marinate in refrigerator 15 to 30 minutes.

In large skillet or wok, heat 1 tablespoon oil over medium-high heat until hot; stir-fry broccoli 1 minute. Add $1/4$ cup broth; cover and cook 1 minute or until crisp-tender. Remove from pan.

In same pan, stir-fry chicken in remaining 1 tablespoon oil 2 to 3 minutes or until no longer pink in center. Combine cornstarch and remaining $1/4$ cup broth, stirring to dissolve. Add cornstarch mixture and broccoli to pan; cook until sauce is thickened and bubbly, stirring occasionally. Sprinkle with sesame seed before serving.

Nutrition information per serving ($1/4$ of recipe): calories 307; total fat 12 g; saturated fat 2 g; cholesterol 63 mg; sodium 520 mg; total carbohydrate 23 g; dietary fiber 4 g; protein 28 g

toasting sesame seed
Accentuate the flavor and aroma of sesame seed by toasting it. Heat a heavy skillet over medium heat until hot. Add sesame seed and toast for 2 to 5 minutes or until seed is lightly browned; stir constantly to prevent burning. Remove from heat.

creamy baked fish

Makes 6 servings   **PREP TIME: 10 minutes**   **COOK/BAKE TIME: 20 minutes**

$1^{1}/_{2}$ pounds fish fillets, approximately $^{1}/_{2}$ inch thick
Seasoning
$1^{1}/_{2}$ teaspoons TONE'S Dill Weed
 $^{3}/_{4}$ teaspoon TONE'S Garlic Salt
 $^{1}/_{4}$ teaspoon TONE'S Ground White Pepper
Sauce
  2 tablespoons butter or margarine
$1^{1}/_{2}$ tablespoons all-purpose flour
 $^{3}/_{4}$ cup milk or half-and-half

In small bowl, combine seasoning ingredients. In oiled baking pan, arrange fish in single layer, overlapping thinner ends of fish to prevent overcooking; sprinkle with $^{1}/_{2}$ of seasoning. Bake at 400°F for 10 minutes.

Meanwhile, prepare sauce. In small saucepan, melt butter over medium heat; stir in flour until smooth. Slowly whisk in milk and remaining $^{1}/_{2}$ of seasoning until smooth; bring to a boil, stirring constantly. Reduce heat; simmer 3 to 4 minutes or until thickened, stirring constantly.

Spoon sauce evenly over fish. Continue baking 10 minutes or until fish flakes when tested.

Nutrition information per serving ($^{1}/_{6}$ of recipe): calories 214; total fat 9 g; saturated fat 4 g; cholesterol 88 mg; sodium 435 mg; total carbohydrate 3 g; dietary fiber 0 g; protein 28 g

spice advice: how fresh is it?

To check for the freshness of herbs and spices in your cupboard, consider the aroma and color of the seasoning. Remove a small amount of the spice or herb from the container and crush it in your hand. It should have a bright, rich color and full aroma. (Whole spices won't release their full fragrance until they are broken or crushed.)

cajun fish

Makes 4 servings   **PREP TIME: 5 minutes**   **COOK TIME: 6 to 10 minutes**

1   pound fish fillets or steaks
1   tablespoon vegetable oil
Seasoning
1   teaspoon TONE'S Garlic Salt
1   teaspoon TONE'S Onion Powder

1   teaspoon TONE'S Spanish Paprika
$^1/_2$ teaspoon TONE'S Oregano (leaves)
$^1/_2$ teaspoon TONE'S Ground Black Pepper
$^1/_4$ to $^1/_2$ teaspoon TONE'S Ground Cayenne Pepper
$^1/_4$ teaspoon TONE'S Ground Thyme

In small bowl, combine seasoning ingredients; press evenly onto both sides of fish. In large heavy skillet, heat oil over medium-high heat until hot; pan-fry fish 6 to 10 minutes or until fish flakes when tested, turning once.

Nutrition information per serving ($^1/_4$ **of recipe):** calories 176; total fat 6 g; saturated fat 1 g; cholesterol 74 mg; sodium 247 mg; total carbohydrate 1 g; dietary fiber 0 g; protein 27 g

broiled deviled fish

Makes 4 servings   **PREP TIME: 10 minutes**   **COOK TIME: 8 to 12 minutes**

1   pound fish fillets or steaks
    Salt and pepper
2   tablespoons grated Parmesan cheese

Seasoning Sauce
$^1/_2$ cup mayonnaise
1   tablespoon Dijon-style mustard
2   teaspoons TONE'S Parsley Flakes or
        2 tablespoons chopped fresh parsley
1   teaspoon TONE'S Oregano (leaves)
$^1/_2$ teaspoon TONE'S Thyme (leaves)

In small bowl, combine seasoning sauce ingredients; set aside. Place fish on oiled rack of broiler pan; season with salt and pepper, as desired. Spread sauce on fish; sprinkle with cheese. Broil 6 inches from heat 8 to 12 minutes or until fish flakes when tested. (Do not turn fish over.)

Nutrition information per serving ($^1/_4$ **of recipe):** calories 370; total fat 27 g; saturated fat 4 g; cholesterol 92 mg; sodium 538 mg; total carbohydrate 2 g; dietary fiber 0 g; protein 29 g

Grilled Salmon with Dill Sauce

grilled salmon
with dill sauce

Makes 6 servings   **PREP TIME: 15 minutes**   **COOK TIME: 8 to 10 minutes**

1 1/2 pounds salmon fillets, skin on
  2 tablespoons vegetable oil
  1 teaspoon TONE'S Onion Powder
1/2 teaspoon freshly ground TONE'S Whole Black Pepper

Dill Sauce
  2 cups plain lowfat yogurt
1/2 cup finely diced seeded peeled cucumber
  2 teaspoons sugar
  2 teaspoons TONE'S Dill Weed
  2 teaspoons fresh lemon juice
  1 teaspoon freshly grated lemon peel
1/4 teaspoon freshly ground TONE'S Whole Black Pepper

In medium bowl, combine dill sauce ingredients; set aside.

Rub both sides of salmon fillets with oil; sprinkle flesh side only with onion powder and pepper. Grill, skin side down, covered, over medium coals 8 to 10 minutes or until salmon flakes when tested. (Do not turn salmon over.) Serve with sauce.

Nutrition information per serving (1/6 of recipe): calories 266; total fat 13 g; saturated fat 3 g; cholesterol 69 mg; sodium 150 mg; total carbohydrate 9 g; dietary fiber 0 g; protein 27 g

RECIPE NOTE: To broil, place salmon on oiled rack in broiler pan, skin side down, so salmon is 3 to 4 inches from heat. Broil 8 to 10 minutes or until salmon flakes when tested. (Do not turn salmon over.)

sole amandine française

MICROWAVE RECIPE
Makes 4 servings   **PREP TIME: 10 minutes**   **COOK TIME: 7 to 12 minutes**

  2 tablespoons butter or margarine
 1/3 cup sliced almonds
  2 tablespoons fresh lemon juice
  1 tablespoon TONE'S Parsley Flakes
        or Chopped Chives
 1/4 to 1/2 teaspoon TONE'S Ground White Pepper
  1 pound sole or other white fish fillets,
        1/4 to 1/2 inch thick
     Salt

In 12 x 8-inch microwave-safe dish, microwave butter on HIGH (100%) 30 to 40 seconds or until melted. (Microwave ovens vary; cooking times may need to be adjusted.) Stir in almonds; cover with wax paper and microwave on HIGH 3 to 5 minutes or until lightly browned, stirring every minute. Using slotted spoon, remove almonds; set aside.

Stir lemon juice, parsley and pepper into butter in dish; add fish, turning to coat. Cover with wax paper; microwave on HIGH 3 to 6 minutes or until fish flakes when tested. Season with salt, as desired; sprinkle with almonds.

Nutrition information per serving (1/4 of recipe): calories 196; total fat 12 g; saturated fat 4 g; cholesterol 69 mg; sodium 276 mg; total carbohydrate 3 g; dietary fiber 1 g; protein 21 g

cook fish just until it's done

When fish is properly cooked, it is opaque and begins to flake easily when the tines of a fork are inserted into the fish and twisted gently. The juices should be milky white. Undercooked fish is translucent and the juices are clear and watery; overcooked fish looks dry and has little or no juices.

grilled shrimp & mango salad

Makes 4 servings
PREP TIME: 20 minutes   **MARINATE TIME: 30 minutes to 12 hours**   **COOK TIME: 4 to 6 minutes**

1 pound medium shrimp, peeled, deveined
  Salt
4 cups thinly sliced romaine lettuce

Salsa
2 large mangoes, peeled, seeded, diced
1 small red onion, finely chopped
2 tablespoons fresh lime juice
1 tablespoon TONE'S Chopped Chives
1 tablespoon olive oil
1/2 teaspoon ground coriander
1/8 teaspoon salt

Marinade
1/2 cup plain lowfat yogurt
1/2 teaspoon ground coriander
1/2 teaspoon TONE'S Ground Cumin Seed
1/2 teaspoon TONE'S Spanish Paprika

In small bowl, combine salsa ingredients; mix well. Cover and refrigerate until ready to serve. In plastic bag, combine marinade ingredients; add shrimp, turning to coat. Close bag securely and marinate in refrigerator 30 minutes to 12 hours.

Remove shrimp from marinade; discard marinade. Thread shrimp onto 8 skewers, dividing evenly. Grill over medium coals 4 to 6 minutes or until shrimp turn pink and are just firm to the touch, turning once. Season with salt, as desired. Place lettuce on 4 plates, dividing evenly. Top each with 2 shrimp kabobs and 1/2 cup salsa.

Nutrition information per serving (1/4 of recipe): calories 189; total fat 5 g; saturated fat 1 g; cholesterol 130 mg; sodium 365 mg; total carbohydrate 16 g; dietary fiber 3 g; protein 20 g

RECIPE NOTE: To broil, place skewered shrimp on rack in broiler pan so surface of shrimp is 2 to 3 inches from heat. Broil 4 to 6 minutes or until done, turning once.

Stir-Fried Shrimp & Snow Peas

44

stir-fried shrimp & snow peas

Makes 4 servings   **PREP TIME: 15 minutes**   **COOK TIME: 8 to 10 minutes**

- 2 tablespoons peanut or vegetable oil, divided
- 3/4 pound medium shrimp, peeled, deveined
- 1/2 pound fresh snow peas, trimmed
- 1/2 cup drained sliced water chestnuts
- 1 tablespoon finely chopped fresh ginger
- 1 tablespoon sesame oil

Seasoning Sauce
- 2 tablespoons soy sauce
- 1 1/2 teaspoons TONE'S Garlic Powder
- 1/4 teaspoon TONE'S Ground White Pepper

In small bowl, combine seasoning sauce ingredients; set aside.

In large skillet or wok, heat 1 tablespoon peanut oil over medium-high heat until hot; stir-fry shrimp 2 to 3 minutes or until shrimp are pink. (Do not overcook.) Remove from pan.

In same pan, stir-fry snow peas, water chestnuts and ginger in remaining 1 tablespoon peanut oil 3 to 4 minutes or until pea pods are crisp-tender. Stir in sauce and shrimp; heat through. Remove from heat; stir in sesame oil. Garnish with green onions, if desired.

Nutrition information per serving (1/4 of recipe): calories 197; total fat 11 g; saturated fat 2 g; cholesterol 121 mg; sodium 495 mg; total carbohydrate 9 g; dietary fiber 2 g; protein 16 g

spice advice: don't get steamed

When adding dried herbs or spices to a mixture, avoid holding the seasoning container over a steaming pot. The steam may cause the seasoning to lose its potency, and the herb or spice may clump in the container. After each use, remember to tightly close the container.

tortellini con melanzane

Makes 4 servings   **PREP TIME: 10 minutes**   **COOK TIME: 25 minutes**

- $1/4$ cup olive oil
- 1 large eggplant ($1^1/4$ to $1^1/2$ pounds), chopped
- 1 medium onion, cut into thin wedges
- 1 can (28 ounces) diced tomatoes, undrained
- 1 to 2 tablespoons finely chopped garlic
- 1 tablespoon TONE'S Italian Seasoning
- 1 teaspoon TONE'S Basil (leaves)
- 1 package (9 ounces) fresh or frozen tortellini
- $1/4$ cup freshly grated Parmesan cheese

In large skillet, heat oil over medium-high heat until hot; cook and stir eggplant and onion 10 minutes. Stir in tomatoes, garlic, Italian seasoning and basil. Reduce heat; cover and simmer 15 minutes or until onion is tender.

Meanwhile cook tortellini as package directs; drain. In large bowl, combine tortellini and eggplant mixture; toss lightly. Sprinkle with cheese.

Nutrition information per serving ($1/4$ of recipe): calories 336; total fat 20 g; saturated fat 5 g; cholesterol 15 mg; sodium 446 mg; total carbohydrate 39 g; dietary fiber 6 g; protein 12 g

broccoli pesto fettuccine

Makes 4 servings   **PREP TIME: 15 minutes**   **COOK TIME: 8 to 10 minutes**

- 8 ounces uncooked fettuccine
  Freshly grated Parmesan cheese
  Pine nuts, toasted (optional)

Broccoli Pesto
- $1^1/2$ cups chopped fresh broccoli
- 1 cup half-and-half
- $1/2$ cup pine nuts, toasted
- $1/4$ cup packed fresh parsley leaves
- 2 tablespoons TONE'S Basil (leaves)
- $1/8$ to $1/4$ teaspoon TONE'S Garlic Powder
  or 1 to 2 cloves garlic
  Salt and pepper

Cook pasta as package directs; drain and keep warm. Meanwhile cook broccoli until tender; drain. In blender or food processor container, combine broccoli, half-and-half, $1/2$ cup pine nuts, parsley, basil and garlic; process until blended. (Thin sauce with additional half-and-half, if desired.) Season with salt and pepper, as desired. In large serving bowl, combine hot pasta and broccoli pesto; toss to coat pasta evenly. Sprinkle with cheese and pine nuts, as desired.

Nutrition information per serving ($^1/_4$ of recipe): calories 445; total fat 19 g; saturated fat 7 g; cholesterol 27 mg; sodium 275 mg; total carbohydrate 55 g; dietary fiber 6 g; protein 18 g

fresh tomato-dill pasta

Makes 4 servings   **PREP TIME: 15 minutes**   **COOK TIME: 10 minutes**

8 ounces uncooked linguine or spaghetti
    Freshly grated Parmesan cheese

Fresh Tomato Sauce

3 medium tomatoes (approximately 1$^1/_2$ pounds), chopped

2 teaspoons TONE'S Parsley Flakes
    or 2 tablespoons finely chopped fresh parsley

2 teaspoons finely chopped green onion

1$^1/_2$ teaspoons TONE'S Dill Weed

$^1/_8$ teaspoon TONE'S Garlic Powder
    or 1 clove garlic, finely chopped

2 tablespoons olive oil
    Salt and pepper

Cook pasta as package directs; drain and keep warm. Meanwhile in large bowl, combine tomatoes, parsley, green onion, dill weed and garlic; stir in oil. Season with salt and pepper, as desired. Add hot pasta; toss to coat. Sprinkle with cheese, as desired.

Nutrition information per serving ($^1/_4$ of recipe): calories 350; total fat 10 g; saturated fat 2 g; cholesterol 5 mg; sodium 269 mg; total carbohydrate 54 g; dietary fiber 4 g; protein 12 g

spice advice: seasoning substitutions

Sometimes, one seasoning can be substituted for another. For example, if your recipe calls for saffron, probably the world's most expensive spice, try a dash of turmeric for color. Or, for dried Italian seasoning, substitute an equal amount of dried basil. Ground allspice and cloves can also be substituted for one another. Try experimenting—you may create a whole new taste sensation.

on the side
from salads to soups to vegetables

Call these recipes "sides," but they take a starring role on any lunch or dinner plate! With Tone's herbs and spices, dressings are distinctive, and sauces superlative, making these accompaniments the highlight of your meals.

Spanish Gazpacho Salad (see recipe, page 50)

spanish gazpacho salad

Makes 4 servings   **PREP TIME: 20 minutes**

1½ cups chopped, seeded tomatoes
¾ cup diced, peeled cucumber
¼ cup chopped green bell pepper
¼ cup chopped green onion

Spanish Dressing (see recipe, below)
4 cups shredded romaine or other lettuce

Combine tomatoes, cucumber, bell pepper and green onion; stir in one-half of dressing. Toss shredded lettuce with remaining dressing; place on serving platter. Mound tomato mixture on lettuce. Garnish with avocado slices and cherry tomatoes, if desired.

Nutrition information per serving (with dressing): calories 155; total fat 14 g; saturated fat 2 g; cholesterol 0 mg; sodium 157 mg; total carbohydrate 8 g; dietary fiber 2 g; protein 2 g

spanish dressing

Makes about ½ cup   **PREP TIME: 5 minutes**

¼ cup SPICE ISLANDS Red Wine Vinegar
2 teaspoons TONE'S Parsley Flakes
1 teaspoon Worcestershire sauce
¼ teaspoon salt

⅛ teaspoon TONE'S Minced Garlic
   or 1 clove garlic, minced
⅛ teaspoon TONE'S Ground Cayenne Pepper
¼ cup olive oil

In small bowl, combine ingredients, slowly stirring in olive oil. Cover and refrigerate until serving time.

Pictured on pages 48–49

sesame spinach salad

Makes 6 servings   **PREP TIME: 15 minutes**

- 6 cups torn spinach leaves
- 1/2 cup fresh or drained canned pineapple chunks
- 1/2 small red onion, sliced, separated into rings
- 1/3 cup sliced radishes
- 1/4 cup Ginger Sesame Dressing (see recipe, below)

In large bowl, combine spinach, pineapple, onion and radishes. Pour dressing over salad; toss lightly to coat.

Nutrition information per serving (1/6 of recipe): calories 85; total fat 7 g; saturated fat 1 g; cholesterol 0 mg; sodium 113 mg; total carbohydrate 6 g; dietary fiber 2 g; protein 2 g

ginger sesame dressing

Makes 1 cup   **PREP TIME: 5 minutes**

- 2/3 cup vegetable oil
- 1/3 cup SPICE ISLANDS White Wine Vinegar
- 2 tablespoons sesame seed, toasted (see tip, page 37)
- 1 1/2 tablespoons sugar
- 1 1/2 teaspoons ground ginger
- 3/4 teaspoon salt
- 1/4 to 1/2 teaspoon TONE'S Crushed Red Pepper
- 1/8 teaspoon TONE'S Ground Black Pepper

In small bowl, combine all ingredients; whisk until blended. Cover and refrigerate until serving time.

Nutrition information per serving (1 tablespoon): calories 92; total fat 9 g; saturated fat 1 g; cholesterol 0 mg; sodium 101 mg; total carbohydrate 2 g; dietary fiber 0 g; protein 0 g

RECIPE NOTE: Use as dressing for Sesame Spinach Salad, mixed green salads or fruit salads. If desired, dressing may be made in a jar with a tight-fitting lid; combine ingredients and shake vigorously. Store dressing in refrigerator.

mediterranean orange &
kalamata salad

Makes 6 servings   **PREP TIME: 15 minutes**

- 6 cups torn mixed salad greens
- 3 large oranges, peeled, chopped
- 1 small red onion, thinly sliced
- $3/4$ cup pitted kalamata olives
  Orange Dressing (see recipe, below)

Arrange salad greens, oranges, onion and olives on individual plates or large platter. Pour dressing evenly over salad just before serving.

Nutrition information per serving ($1/6$ of recipe): calories 237; total fat 18 g; saturated fat 2 g; cholesterol 0 mg; sodium 756 mg; total carbohydrate 19 g; dietary fiber 5 g; protein 3 g

orange dressing

Makes about $1/2$ cup   **PREP TIME: 5 minutes**

- $1/3$ cup olive oil
- 2 tablespoons orange juice
- 2 tablespoons SPICE ISLANDS Balsamic Vinegar
- $1/2$ teaspoon salt
- $1/4$ teaspoon ground coriander
- $1/4$ teaspoon TONE'S Ground Black Pepper
- $1/8$ teaspoon ground cloves

In small bowl, combine dressing ingredients; whisk until blended. Cover and refrigerate until serving time.

greens & grapes

Makes 6 servings   **PREP TIME: 10 minutes**

6 cups torn salad greens
1 cup seedless red grapes

$1/2$ cup Balsamic Vinaigrette
    (see recipe, below)
$1/4$ cup freshly shaved Parmesan cheese
    (approximately 1 ounce)

In large bowl, combine greens and grapes. Add vinaigrette; toss lightly to coat. Top with cheese.

Nutrition information per serving ($1/6$ of recipe): calories 158; total fat 14 g; saturated fat 3 g; cholesterol 3 mg; sodium 169 mg; total carbohydrate 8 g; dietary fiber 1 g; protein 3 g

balsamic vinaigrette

Makes 1$1/2$ cups   **PREP TIME: 5 minutes**

1 cup olive oil
$1/3$ cup SPICE ISLANDS Balsamic Vinegar
2 tablespoons coarse grain mustard
1 teaspoon TONE'S Parsley Flakes
    or 1 tablespoon chopped fresh parsley

1 teaspoon TONE'S Chopped Chives
$1/4$ teaspoon TONE'S Garlic Powder
    or 2 cloves garlic, finely chopped
Salt and pepper (optional)

In medium bowl, combine all ingredients; whisk until blended. Cover and refrigerate until serving time.

Nutrition information per serving (1 tablespoon): calories 84; total fat 9 g; saturated fat 1 g; cholesterol 0 mg; sodium 65 mg; total carbohydrate 1 g; dietary fiber 0 g; protein 0 g

RECIPE NOTE: Use as dressing for Greens & Grapes or mixed green salads. If desired, vinaigrette may be made in a jar with a tight-fitting lid; combine ingredients and shake vigorously. Store vinaigrette in refrigerator. Olive oil mixture will solidify, so allow to stand at room temperature 10 minutes, then shake.

avocado olé

Makes 6 servings   **PREP TIME: 15 minutes**

2   medium avocados, pitted, peeled, diced
    (approximately 2 cups)
1   can (15 ounces) kidney beans, rinsed, drained
1   cup pitted ripe olives, drained

2   tablespoons chopped green onion
1/3 cup Olé Dressing (see recipe, below)
4   cups torn green leaf or other lettuce

In large bowl, combine avocados, beans, olives and green onion. Add dressing; toss lightly to coat. Place lettuce on platter; top with avocado mixture.

Nutrition information per serving (1/6 of recipe): calories 409; total fat 30 g; saturated fat 7 g; cholesterol 14 mg; sodium 696 mg; total carbohydrate 29 g; dietary fiber 10 g; protein 9 g

RECIPE NOTE: For a taco salad variation, serve Avocado Olé in prepared taco shells; garnish with sour cream and shredded cheddar cheese.

olé dressing

Makes 3/4 cup   **PREP TIME: 5 minutes**

1/2 cup olive or vegetable oil
1/4 cup SPICE ISLANDS Red Wine Vinegar
    (Garlic or regular flavor)
1   teaspoon sugar

1   teaspoon TONE'S Chili Powder
1/2 teaspoon salt
1/2 teaspoon TONE'S Ground Cumin Seed

In small bowl, combine all ingredients; whisk until blended. Cover and refrigerate until serving time.

Nutrition information per serving (1 tablespoon): calories 88; total fat 9 g; saturated fat 1 g; cholesterol 0 mg; sodium 91 mg; total carbohydrate 1 g; dietary fiber 0 g; protein 0 g

RECIPE NOTE: Use as dressing for Avocado Olé or mixed greens. If desired, dressing may be made in a jar with a tight-fitting lid; combine ingredients and shake vigorously. Store dressing in refrigerator. Olive oil mixture will solidify, so allow to stand at room temperature 10 minutes, then shake.

french potato salad

Makes 6 servings   **PREP TIME: 15 minutes**   **COOK TIME: 15 to 20 minutes**

4 cups sliced (¼ inch thick) unpeeled red
    potatoes (approximately 1½ pounds)
   Salt (optional)

½ cup sliced celery
¼ cup finely chopped green onions
½ cup Tarragon Dijon Vinaigrette
    (see recipe, below)

In medium saucepan, combine potatoes with cold water to cover; add salt, if desired. Bring to a boil; reduce heat. Cover and simmer 12 to 15 minutes or until tender; drain. In large bowl, combine potatoes, celery and green onions. Add vinaigrette; toss lightly to coat. Serve warm or at room temperature.

Nutrition information per serving (⅙ of recipe): calories 184; total fat 9 g; saturated fat 1 g; cholesterol 0 mg; sodium 224 mg; total carbohydrate 23 g; dietary fiber 3 g; protein 3 g

RECIPE NOTE: For variety, add 1 cup cooked diagonally-cut green beans to the potato salad; toss lightly.

tarragon dijon vinaigrette

Makes 1 cup   **PREP TIME: 5 minutes**

½ cup olive or vegetable oil
½ cup SPICE ISLANDS White Wine Vinegar
    (Tarragon or regular flavor)
1 tablespoon Dijon-style mustard

2 teaspoons tarragon
1 teaspoon salt
¼ to ½ teaspoon TONE'S Ground Black Pepper

In small bowl, combine all ingredients; whisk until blended. Cover and refrigerate until serving time.

Nutrition information per serving (1 tablespoon): calories 64; total fat 7 g; saturated fat 1 g; cholesterol 0 mg; sodium 157 mg; total carbohydrate 0 g; dietary fiber 0 g; protein 0 g

RECIPE NOTE: Use as dressing for French Potato Salad or mixed greens with chicken or seafood. If desired, vinaigrette may be made in a jar with a tight-fitting lid; combine ingredients and shake vigorously. Store vinaigrette in refrigerator. Olive oil mixture will solidify, so allow to stand at room temperature 10 minutes, then shake.

italian tomato soup

MICROWAVE RECIPE
Makes 4 servings

PREP TIME: 10 minutes

COOK TIME: 20 MINUTES

- 1 tablespoon olive oil
- ½ cup diced carrot
- ½ cup diced onion
- 1 can (28 ounces) peeled tomatoes, ready-cut and undrained or 3 cups diced, peeled and seeded fresh tomatoes

- Water
- 2 tablespoons tomato paste
- 1½ teaspoons TONE'S Italian Seasoning
- Yogurt or sour cream (optional)
- Sage Croutons (see recipe, below)

In large 2- to 3-quart microwave-safe bowl, combine oil, carrot and onion. Cover and microwave on HIGH (100%) 6 to 8 minutes, stirring once, until vegetables are just tender. (Microwave ovens vary; cooking times may need to be adjusted.) Add enough water to tomatoes and reserved liquid to make 3½ cups. Stir tomato mixture, tomato paste and Italian seasoning into bowl. Cover; microwave on HIGH 3 to 4 minutes or until hot. Top each serving with a dollop of yogurt or sour cream and Sage Croutons.

SAGE CROUTONS: Trim crusts from 4 thin slices of sandwich bread. Combine 2 tablespoons olive oil with 2 cloves garlic, minced. Brush on bread slices. Cut each slice into 4 triangles. Sprinkle with ½ teaspoon TONE'S Ground Sage (rubbed). Arrange 4 croutons in a circle on microwave-safe pie plate. Microwave on HIGH for 30 seconds to 1 minute. Repeat with remaining croutons. Makes 16.

Nutrition information per serving (¼ of recipe): calories 221; total fat 12 g; saturated fat 2 g; cholesterol 0 mg; sodium 475 mg; total carbohydrate 27 g; dietary fiber 3 g; protein 5 g

Italian Tomato Soup

chilled avocado soup

Makes 4 servings　　　　**PREP TIME: 10 minutes**　　　　**CHILL TIME: 1 hour or overnight**

- 1 large avocado, pitted, peeled
- 1 can (14½ ounces) ready-to-serve chicken broth
- ¼ cup plain lowfat yogurt
- 1 tablespoon fresh lime juice
- ½ teaspoon ground coriander
- ½ teaspoon TONE'S Ground Cumin Seed
- ¼ teaspoon salt
- 1 tablespoon finely chopped green onion
- ½ teaspoon TONE'S Crushed Red Pepper
  Chopped fresh tomatoes, sliced green onion and crushed tortilla chips

In blender or food processor container, combine avocado, broth, yogurt, lime juice, coriander, cumin and salt; process until mixture is smooth. Add green onion and crushed red pepper; pulse on and off until just combined. Cover and refrigerate 1 hour or overnight. To serve, top with tomatoes, onion and tortilla chips, as desired.

Nutrition information per serving (¼ of recipe): calories 148; total fat 11 g; saturated fat 2 g; cholesterol 1 mg; sodium 528 mg; total carbohydrate 11 g; dietary fiber 4 g; protein 5 g

dill potato soup

Makes 4 servings　　　　**PREP TIME: 15 minutes**　　　　**COOK TIME: 25 minutes**

- 2 tablespoons butter or margarine
- 1 cup chopped onion
- 2 cups cubed peeled potatoes (approximately 2 medium)
- 2 cups water
- 4 teaspoons TONE'S Chicken Soup Base
- ⅛ teaspoon TONE'S Garlic Powder
- ½ cup half-and-half
- 1 teaspoon TONE'S Dill Weed
  Salt and pepper

In saucepan, heat butter over medium-high heat until hot; cook and stir onion 3 to 5 minutes or until tender. Add potatoes, water, soup base, and garlic powder; bring to a boil. Reduce heat; simmer 12 to 15 minutes or until potatoes are tender. Transfer to blender or food processor container; process until smooth. Return to pan; heat to simmering. Remove from heat; stir in half-and-half and dill weed. Season with salt and pepper, as desired. Serve hot or chilled.

Nutrition information per serving (approximately 1 cup): calories 178; total fat 10 g; saturated fat 6 g; cholesterol 29 mg; sodium 623 mg; total carbohydrate 20 g; dietary fiber 2 g; protein 3 g

Springtime Carrots with Herbs

springtime carrots with herbs

Makes 4 servings   **PREP TIME: 12 minutes**   **COOK TIME: 10 to 14 minutes**

1 pound carrots, cut into thin sticks	1 tablespoon packed brown sugar
1/3 cup water	1 teaspoon TONE'S Rosemary (leaves), crushed
Glaze	1 teaspoon TONE'S Thyme (leaves)
3 tablespoons butter or margarine	1/4 teaspoon salt
2 tablespoons dry sherry	

In medium skillet, combine carrots and water; bring to a boil. Reduce heat to medium-low; cover and simmer 4 to 6 minutes or until crisp-tender, adding more water if necessary. Drain carrots. In same skillet, combine carrots with glaze ingredients. Cook, uncovered, 4 to 6 minutes or until carrots are glazed, stirring frequently.

Nutrition information per serving (1/4 **of recipe**): calories 143; total fat 9 g; saturated fat 5 g; cholesterol 23 mg; sodium 292 mg; total carbohydrate 15 g; dietary fiber 3 g; protein 1 g

quick chard sauté

Makes 4 servings   **PREP TIME: 10 minutes**   **COOK TIME: 8 to 10 minutes**

1 tablespoon vegetable oil	1 tablespoons sesame seed, toasted (see tip, page 37)
6 cups sliced Swiss chard (1 medium head)	2 teaspoons soy sauce
1/4 teaspoon TONE'S Minced Garlic	

In large skillet, heat oil over medium heat until hot. Cook and stir Swiss chard and garlic 5 to 6 minutes or until tender and liquid is evaporated. Remove from heat; stir in sesame seed and soy sauce.

Nutrition information per serving (1/4 **of recipe**): calories 57; total fat 5 g; saturated fat 1 g; cholesterol 0 mg; sodium 181 mg; total carbohydrate 3 g; dietary fiber 1 g; protein 2 g

calabacitas
(little squash)

Makes 4 servings   **PREP TIME: 15 minutes**   **COOK TIME: 10 minutes**

- 1 tablespoon vegetable oil
- 1 pound zucchini, cut into $1/4$-inch-thick slices
- $1/2$ pound crookneck squash, cut into $1/4$-inch-thick slices
- $3/4$ teaspoon TONE'S Garlic Powder or 1 tablespoon finely chopped garlic
- 1 package (10 ounces) frozen whole kernel corn, thawed
- 1 can (4 ounces) diced mild green chiles
- 2 teaspoons TONE'S Ground Cumin Seed
- 1 teaspoon TONE'S Basil (leaves)
- $1/4$ teaspoon TONE'S Ground Cayenne Pepper
- Salt

In large skillet, heat oil over medium-high heat until hot. Add zucchini, crookneck squash and chopped garlic, if used; cook and stir 4 to 5 minutes or until vegetables are crisp-tender. Add corn, chiles, cumin, basil, cayenne pepper and garlic powder, if used; cook and stir 5 minutes or until mixture is heated through and flavors are blended. Season with salt, as desired.

Nutrition information per serving ($1/4$ of recipe): calories 125; total fat 4 g; saturated fat 1 g; cholesterol 0 mg; sodium 475 mg; total carbohydrate 23 g; dietary fiber 4 g; protein 4 g

supper with a mexican flair

Accompany roast pork with an Avocado Olé salad (see recipe, page 54) and Calabacitas as the vegetable side dish. Pass a basket of tortillas with the meal and serve rice pudding spiced with cinnamon for dessert.

chinese sweet & sour vegetables

Makes 6 to 8 servings   **PREP TIME: 15 minutes**   **COOK TIME: 10 minutes**

- 1 tablespoon vegetable oil
- 1 carrot, cut diagonally into $1/4$-inch-thick slices
- 1 medium onion, cut into 1-inch pieces
- 4 cups sliced green cabbage or Chinese cabbage
- 1 green or red bell pepper, cut into 1-inch pieces
- 1 cup fresh or drained canned pineapple chunks
- 1 tablespoon sesame seed, toasted
     (optional) (see tip, page 37)

Sauce
- $1/4$ cup sugar
- $1/4$ cup catsup
- $1/4$ cup SPICE ISLANDS Red Wine Vinegar
     (Garlic or regular flavor)
- $1/4$ cup water
- 1 tablespoon soy sauce
- 1 teaspoon arrowroot or TONE'S Cornstarch
- $1/2$ teaspoon ground ginger
- $1/8$ teaspoon TONE'S Garlic Powder
     or 1 clove garlic, finely chopped

In large skillet or wok, heat oil over medium-high heat until hot; stir-fry carrot and onion 2 minutes. Add cabbage and bell pepper; stir-fry 3 to 5 minutes or until vegetables are crisp-tender. Transfer to large bowl.

In small saucepan, combine sauce ingredients; bring to a boil over medium heat, stirring constantly. Reduce heat; simmer 1 to 2 minutes or until thickened, stirring occasionally.

Add pineapple and sauce to cooked vegetables; toss lightly. Sprinkle with sesame seed, if desired.

Nutrition information per serving ($1/6$ of recipe): calories 121; total fat 3 g; saturated fat 0 g; cholesterol 0 mg; sodium 213 mg; total carbohydrate 23 g; dietary fiber 4 g; protein 2 g

tuscan green beans

Makes 4 servings   **PREP TIME: 10 minutes**   **COOK TIME: 15 minutes**

1   pound fresh or frozen green beans
Sauce
3   tablespoons olive or vegetable oil
1   ounce sliced salami, cut into thin strips
     (approximately $^1/_4$ cup)

1   clove garlic, finely chopped
1   large tomato, chopped
2   tablespoons SPICE ISLANDS
     Red Wine Vinegar
1   teaspoon TONE'S Oregano (leaves)
     Salt and pepper

Cook green beans, as desired, until crisp-tender; drain. Transfer to serving bowl; set aside and keep warm. Meanwhile in medium skillet, heat oil over medium heat until hot; cook and stir salami and garlic 3 to 4 minutes or until garlic is golden. Stir in tomato, vinegar and oregano; cook until sauce is hot, stirring occasionally. Season with salt and pepper, as desired. Pour sauce over beans; serve immediately.

Nutrition information per serving ($^1/_4$ of recipe): calories 168; total fat 13 g; saturated fat 2 g; cholesterol 6 mg; sodium 273 mg; total carbohydrate 11 g; dietary fiber 4 g; protein 4 g

oriental rice pilaf

Makes 4 to 6 servings   **PREP TIME: 5 minutes**   **COOK TIME: 25 minutes**

2   teaspoons sesame oil or vegetable oil
1   cup uncooked long grain white rice
1   can (10$^1/_2$ ounces) condensed chicken broth
$^1/_2$ cup water

1   tablespoon soy sauce
1   teaspoon TONE'S Garlic Powder
$^1/_2$ teaspoon ground ginger
$^1/_4$ cup sliced green onions

In medium saucepan, heat oil over medium heat until hot; cook and stir rice 3 to 5 minutes or until golden. Stir in broth, water, soy sauce, garlic powder and ginger; bring to a boil. Reduce heat to low; cover and simmer 20 minutes or until liquid is absorbed and rice is tender. Stir in green onions.

Nutrition information per serving ($^1/_4$ of recipe): calories 236; total fat 4 g; saturated fat 1 g; cholesterol 1 mg; sodium 581 mg; total carbohydrate 42 g; dietary fiber 1 g; protein 8 g

Tuscan Green Beans

herb-baked potato wedges

Makes 4 servings   **PREP TIME: 5 minutes**   **BAKE TIME: 50 to 60 minutes**

- 4 medium potatoes (approximately 2 pounds),
     each cut lengthwise into 8 wedges

Seasoning
- 3 tablespoons vegetable or olive oil
- 2 tablespoons SPICE ISLANDS Garlic
     Red Wine Vinegar
- 1 teaspoon TONE'S Oregano (leaves)
- 1 teaspoon TONE'S Rosemary (leaves), crushed
- $1/2$ teaspoon salt
- $1/8$ to $1/4$ teaspoon TONE'S Ground Black Pepper

In 13 x 9-inch baking pan, combine seasoning ingredients. Add potatoes; toss to coat. Bake at 400°F for 50 to 60 minutes or until potatoes are tender and lightly browned, stirring occasionally.

Nutrition information per serving ($1/4$ of recipe): calories 296; total fat 11 g; saturated fat 2 g; cholesterol 0 mg; sodium 282 mg; total carbohydrate 47 g; dietary fiber 5 g; protein 4 g

spice advice: using dried herbs

Measure the correct amount of herb needed, then crush leaf herbs to release the aromatic oils before adding to the food. Use your fingers and the palm of your hand, or rub between your fingers or use a mortar and pestle for crushing. If you add herbs at the beginning of cooking, the flavors will be more blended; adding them at the end will lend a more distinctive flavor.

rosemary new potatoes

Makes 4 servings **PREP TIME: 10 minutes** **BAKE TIME: 1 hour**

- ¼ cup olive oil
- 1 tablespoon Dijon-style mustard
- 1½ teaspoons TONE'S Spanish Paprika
- ¼ teaspoon TONE'S Garlic Powder
      or 2 cloves garlic, sliced
- ¼ teaspoon salt
- 1 tablespoon TONE'S Rosemary (leaves), crushed
- 2 pounds new red potatoes, cut in half
      (quartered, if large)

In blender or food processor container, combine oil, mustard, paprika, garlic and salt; process until smooth. Add rosemary; pulse on and off just until blended.

In 13 x 9-inch baking pan, combine potatoes and oil mixture; toss to coat. Spread potatoes in even layer. Bake at 400°F for 1 hour or until potatoes are tender and lightly browned, stirring occasionally.

Nutrition information per serving (¼ of recipe): calories 332; total fat 14 g; saturated fat 2 g; cholesterol 0 mg; sodium 244 mg; total carbohydrate 48 g; dietary fiber 5 g; protein 5 g

spice advice: experimenting with seasonings

If you want to experiment using Tone's herbs and spices in your own recipes, start with ¼ teaspoon per 4 servings or one pound of meat. When using cayenne or garlic powder, start with ⅛ teaspoon. Also note that cayenne intensifies when cooked, so start with smaller amounts of this seasoning.

home-baked breads
for mealtime enjoyment
or gift giving

From the moment these breads begin

to bake and the aroma of Tone's spices

and herbs fills your kitchen, you'll

know home-baked breads are worth

the time! For a sweet breakfast treat,

a partner for pasta or a homemade

housewarming gift, these breads

go anywhere and are irresistible

anytime.

Cranberry Bread (see recipe, page 68)

cranberry bread

Makes 1 large or 4 small loaves
PREP TIME: 15 minutes   BAKE TIME: 55 to 65 minutes (large loaf)

$^1/_2$ cup (1 stick) butter or margarine, softened
$1^1/_3$ cups sugar
  2 eggs
  1 tablespoon freshly grated orange peel
  2 teaspoons TONE'S Pure Vanilla Extract
$2^1/_2$ cups self-rising flour
$1^1/_2$ teaspoons TONE'S Ground Cinnamon
 $^3/_4$ cup milk
$1^1/_2$ cups fresh or frozen cranberries

Using electric mixer, in large bowl, beat butter and sugar until light and creamy; beat in eggs, orange peel and vanilla. Combine flour and cinnamon; beat into butter mixture alternately with milk until blended. Fold in cranberries.

Spoon into greased and floured 9 x 5-inch loaf pan or four $5^3/_4$ x $3^1/_4$ x 2-inch foil loaf pans. Bake at 350°F for 55 to 65 minutes for large loaf (45 to 55 minutes for small loaves) or until wooden pick inserted into center comes out clean. Cool in pan on wire rack 15 minutes. Remove from pan; cool completely on wire rack.

Nutrition information per serving ($^1/_{16}$ of recipe): calories 206; total fat 7 g; saturated fat 4 g; cholesterol 43 mg; sodium 320 mg; total carbohydrate 34 g; dietary fiber 3 g; protein 3 g

Pictured on pages 66–67

spiced pumpkin bread
with orange cream cheese

Makes 1 loaf   **PREP TIME: 15 minutes**   **BAKE TIME: 1 to 1 1/4 hours**

- 1/3 cup (2/3 stick) butter or margarine, softened
- 1 1/4 cups sugar
- 1 cup solid pack pumpkin
- 1 egg
- 1 3/4 cups all-purpose flour
- 1 teaspoon TONE'S Ground Cinnamon
- 1/2 teaspoon baking soda
- 1/2 teaspoon salt

- 1/4 teaspoon TONE'S Baking Powder
- 1/4 teaspoon ground ginger
- 1/4 teaspoon ground allspice
- 1/8 teaspoon TONE's Ground Nutmeg
- 1/2 cup dried currants
- 1/2 cup chopped pecans
- Orange Cream Cheese (see recipe, below)

Using electric mixer, beat butter and sugar until light; add pumpkin and egg, mixing well. In medium bowl, combine flour, cinnamon, baking soda, salt, baking powder, ginger, allspice and nutmeg; gradually add to butter mixture, mixing until well blended. Stir in currants and pecans.

Pour batter into greased 8 x 4-inch loaf pan. Bake at 350°F for 1 to 1 1/4 hours or until wooden pick inserted into center comes out clean. Cool in pan on wire rack 15 minutes. Remove from pan; cool completely on wire rack. Serve with Orange Cream Cheese.

ORANGE CREAM CHEESE: In medium bowl, combine 1 package (8 ounces) cream cheese, softened; 3 tablespoons sugar; 2 teaspoons TONE'S Pure Vanilla Extract and 1 teaspoon freshly grated orange peel. Stir until smooth. Stir in 1 to 2 teaspoons milk to make spreading consistency.

Nutrition information per serving (1/16 **of recipe**): calories 250; total fat 12 g; saturated fat 6 g; cholesterol 39 mg; sodium 198 mg; total carbohydrate 34 g; dietary fiber 1 g; protein 4 g

gifts from the kitchen
For gift giving, place a loaf of wrapped bread in a decorative basket along with a container of Orange Cream Cheese. Wrap the entire gift with cellophane and add a colorful bow and gift tag. This makes an ideal hostess gift during the holidays or whenever you need a home-baked treat.

Zucchini Raisin Wheat Muffins

zucchini raisin wheat muffins

Makes 12 muffins   **PREP TIME: 20 minutes**   **BAKE TIME: 20 to 25 minutes**

- 1/2 cup butter or margarine, softened
- 1/2 cup packed brown sugar
- 2 eggs, beaten
- 1/4 cup milk
- 1 cup all-purpose flour
- 1 cup whole wheat flour
- 2 teaspoons TONE'S Baking Powder
- 1 teaspoon TONE'S Ground Cinnamon
- 1/2 teaspoon salt
- 1/8 teaspoon ground cloves
- 1 1/2 cups finely shredded zucchini
- 1/2 cup snipped golden raisins or currants

Using electric mixer, in large mixing bowl, beat butter and sugar until light and fluffy. Add eggs, one at a time, beating until combined. Beat in milk. In medium bowl, combine flours, baking powder, cinnamon, salt and cloves; add to butter mixture. Stir in zucchini until combined. Stir in raisins or currants.

Spoon batter into 12 greased 2 1/2-inch muffin cups, filling each almost full. Bake at 375°F for 20 to 25 minutes or until golden. Cool in muffin cups on wire rack 5 minutes. Remove from muffin cups and serve warm.

Nutrition information per muffin: calories 203; total fat 9 g; saturated fat 5 g; cholesterol 56 mg; sodium 244 mg; total carbohydrate 28 g; dietary fiber 2 g; protein 4 g

RECIPE NOTE: These extra-moist, hearty muffins can be baked in paper bake cup-lined muffin pans or in greased muffin pans.

cinnamon streusel scones

Makes 8 scones   **PREP TIME: 15 minutes**   **BAKE TIME: 20 to 25 minutes**

2 cups all-purpose flour
1/4 cup granulated sugar
1 tablespoon TONE'S Baking Powder
1/4 teaspoon salt
1/2 cup (1 stick) butter or margarine
2 eggs, beaten
1/3 cup whipping cream

Filling

1/2 cup dried currants or raisins
6 tablespoons packed brown sugar
2 tablespoons butter or margarine, melted
1 teaspoon TONE'S Ground Cinnamon
1/4 teaspoon TONE'S Ground Nutmeg

Topping

1 egg white, lightly beaten
2 teaspoons granulated sugar
1/4 teaspoon TONE'S Ground Cinnamon

In small bowl, combine filling ingredients; set aside. In large bowl, combine flour, 1/4 cup granulated sugar, baking powder and salt. Cut in butter until mixture resembles coarse crumbs. With fork, stir in eggs and cream until just moistened. On lightly floured surface, knead gently 8 to 10 times.

Divide dough in half; pat each into a 6-inch circle, about 1 inch thick. Place one circle on ungreased baking sheet; spread filling evenly on circle to within 1/2 inch of edge. Top with second circle; gently press edges to seal.

Brush top with egg white. Combine 2 teaspoons granulated sugar and 1/4 teaspoon cinnamon; sprinkle over top. Cutting through top layer only, cut into 8 wedges. Bake at 400°F for 20 to 25 minutes or until golden brown. Cut into 8 scones; serve warm.

Nutrition information per serving (1 scone): calories 370; total fat 20 g; saturated fat 12 g; cholesterol 105 mg; sodium 427 mg; total carbohydrate 44 g; dietary fiber 2 g; protein 6 g

focaccia

Makes 6 servings
PREP TIME: 15 minutes   **REST/PROOF TIME: 25 to 40 minutes**   **BAKE TIME: 25 minutes**

2³/₄ cups all-purpose flour
  1 package (2¹/₄ teaspoons) FLEISCHMANN'S
      RapidRise Yeast
2¹/₂ teaspoons TONE'S Oregano (leaves)
 ¹/₂ teaspoon salt
  1 cup very warm water (120 to 130°F)
  2 tablespoons olive oil
  1 egg
Topping
      Onion and Herb Topping or Parmesan and Pecan
          Topping (see recipes, below)

In large bowl, combine 1¹/₂ cups flour, undissolved yeast, oregano and salt. Stir in water and oil. Stir in egg and enough remaining flour to make stiff batter. Cover; let rest 10 minutes.

With lightly oiled hands, spread batter in oiled 13 x 9-inch baking pan. Prepare topping as directed; add topping. Cover loosely with plastic wrap; let rise in warm, draft-free place until almost doubled in size, about 15 to 30 minutes.

Remove plastic wrap. Bake at 400°F for 25 minutes or until done. Cool in pan on wire rack or serve warm.

ONION AND HERB TOPPING: In large skillet, cook 1¹/₂ cups thinly sliced onions in ¹/₄ cup olive oil over medium heat 3 to 4 minutes or until onion is soft but not browned, stirring occasionally. Spread on top of batter. Sprinkle with 1 teaspoon TONE'S Rosemary (leaves), crushed and 1 teaspoon coarse salt, if desired.
Nutrition information per serving (¹/₆ of focaccia with topping): calories 378; total fat 17 g; saturated fat 3 g; cholesterol 35 mg; sodium 209 mg; total carbohydrate 47 g; dietary fiber 2 g; protein 8 g

PARMESAN AND PECAN TOPPING: Drizzle ¹/₄ cup olive oil over batter. Sprinkle with ³/₄ cup chopped pecans and ¹/₄ cup grated Parmesan cheese; press nuts into batter.
Nutrition information per serving (¹/₆ of focaccia with topping): calories 482; total fat 28 g; saturated fat 4 g; cholesterol 38 mg; sodium 280 mg; total carbohydrate 48 g; dietary fiber 3 g; protein 10 g

dilly bread

Makes 1 loaf
PREP TIME: 20 minutes   **REST/PROOF TIME: 50 to 60 minutes**   **BAKE TIME: 25 minutes**

- 2 cups all-purpose flour
- 1 package (2$\frac{1}{4}$ teaspoons) FLEISCHMANN'S Active Dry Yeast
- 2 teaspoons dill seed
- $\frac{1}{4}$ teaspoon baking soda

- 1 cup cream-style cottage cheese
- $\frac{1}{4}$ cup water
- 2 tablespoons sugar
- 1 tablespoon margarine or butter
- 2 teaspoons TONE'S Dried Chopped Onion
- $\frac{1}{2}$ teaspoon salt
- 1 egg

In large bowl, combine $\frac{3}{4}$ cup flour, undissolved yeast, dill seed and baking soda. In medium saucepan, heat and stir cottage cheese, water, sugar, margarine, onion and salt until warm (120 to 130°F). Stir into dry ingredients. Stir in egg. Beat with electric mixer on low speed for 30 seconds. Beat on high speed 3 minutes. Stir in remaining flour.

Spread batter in a generously greased 1$\frac{1}{2}$-quart soufflé dish or casserole or 9x1$\frac{1}{2}$-inch round baking pan. Cover; let rise in warm, draft-free place until almost doubled in size, about 50 to 60 minutes.

Bake at 375°F about 25 minutes or until golden brown. If necessary, cover with foil the last 10 minutes of baking to prevent overbrowning. Immediately remove from dish or pan. Serve warm or cool on wire rack.

Nutrition information per serving ($\frac{1}{16}$ of recipe): calories 86; total fat 2 g; saturated fat 1 g; cholesterol 15 mg; sodium 152 mg; total carbohydrate 13 g; dietary fiber 1 g; protein 4 g

Dilly Bread

potato rosemary rolls

Makes 12 rolls
PREP TIME: 20 minutes   **REST/PROOF TIME: 30 to 50 minutes**   **BAKE TIME: 15 to 20 minutes**

$2^3/_4$ to $3^1/_4$ cups all-purpose flour
   1 package ($2^1/_4$ teaspoons) FLEISCHMANN'S
          RapidRise Yeast
   1 tablespoon sugar
   2 teaspoons TONE'S Minced Onions
   1 teaspoon salt
   1 teaspoon TONE'S Rosemary (leaves), crushed
  $^3/_4$ cup milk
  $^1/_2$ cup instant potato flakes or buds
  $^1/_2$ cup water
   2 tablespoons olive oil
Topping
   1 egg, lightly beaten
      TONE'S Rosemary (leaves), crushed

   In large bowl, combine $1^1/_2$ cups flour, undissolved yeast, sugar, onions, salt and 1 teaspoon rosemary. Heat milk, potato flakes, water and oil until very warm (120 to 130°F). Stir into dry ingredients. Stir in enough remaining flour to make soft dough. Knead on lightly floured surface until smooth and elastic, about 4 to 6 minutes. Cover; let the dough rest 10 minutes.

   Divide dough into 12 equal pieces. Roll each piece into 10-inch rope; tie loose knot in center of each rope. Place rolls, 2 inches apart, on greased large baking sheet. Cover; let rise in warm, draft-free place until rolls are doubled in size, about 20 to 40 minutes.

   Brush tops with egg. Sprinkle with rosemary as desired. Bake at 375°F for 15 to 20 minutes or until done. Remove from baking sheet; cool on wire rack.

Nutrition information per serving (1 roll): calories 163; total fat 4 g; saturated fat 1 g; cholesterol 10 mg; sodium 209 mg; total carbohydrate 28 g; dietary fiber 1 g; protein 5 g

garden herb loaf

Makes 1 loaf
PREP TIME: 25 minutes   **REST/PROOF TIME: 30 to 50 minutes**   **BAKE TIME: 30 to 35 minutes**

- 4 to 4^{1}/$_{2}$ cups all-purpose flour
- 3 tablespoons sugar
- 2 packages (4^{1}/$_{2}$ teaspoons) FLEISCHMANN'S RapidRise Yeast
- 1^{1}/$_{2}$ teaspoons salt
- ^{3}/$_{4}$ teaspoon marjoram
- ^{3}/$_{4}$ teaspoon TONE'S Rosemary (leaves), crushed
- ^{3}/$_{4}$ teaspoon TONE'S Thyme (leaves)
- ^{3}/$_{4}$ cup milk
- ^{1}/$_{2}$ cup water
- ^{1}/$_{4}$ cup (^{1}/$_{2}$ stick) butter or margarine, cut up
- 1 egg

Topping
- 1 tablespoon butter or margarine, melted
  TONE'S Rosemary (leaves) and Thyme (leaves) (optional)

In large bowl, combine 1^{1}/$_{2}$ cups flour, sugar, undissolved yeast, salt and ^{3}/$_{4}$ teaspoon each marjoram, rosemary and thyme. Heat milk, water and cut up butter until very warm (120 to 130°F); butter does not need to melt. Stir into dry ingredients. Stir in egg and enough remaining flour to make soft dough. Knead on lightly floured surface until smooth and elastic, about 4 to 6 minutes. Cover; let rest 10 minutes.

Divide dough into 3 equal pieces; roll each piece into 30-inch rope. Braid ropes, pinching ends to seal. Tie knot in center of braid. Wrap ends in opposite directions around knot to make round loaf; tuck ends under. Place on greased large baking sheet. Cover; let rise in warm, draft-free place until doubled in size, about 20 to 40 minutes.

Bake at 375°F for 30 to 35 minutes or until done, covering with aluminum foil during last 10 minutes to prevent overbrowning. Brush with melted butter; sprinkle with rosemary and thyme, if desired. Remove from baking sheet; cool on wire rack.

Nutrition information per serving (^{1}/$_{16}$ of recipe): calories 176; total fat 5 g; saturated fat 3 g; cholesterol 24 mg; sodium 267 mg; total carbohydrate 29 g; dietary fiber 1 g; protein 5 g

sweet conclusions

and memorable treats

Sweet tooths will be oh-so-satisfied with these wonderfully grand creations. From Cardamom Biscotti to Hazelnut Chiffon Cake with Mocha Buttercream, gourmet delicacies are luscious and inviting—and particularly flavorful when you use Tone's spices and flavorings.

Pumpkin Pie (see recipe, page 80)

pumpkin pie

Makes 8 servings   **PREP TIME: 25 minutes**   **BAKE TIME: 50 minutes**

1 can (15 ounces) solid pack pumpkin	3 slightly beaten eggs
²/₃ cup sugar	1 can (5 ounces) evaporated milk
1 teaspoons TONE'S Ground Cinnamon	¹/₂ cup milk
¹/₂ teaspoon TONE'S Ground Nutmeg	1 unbaked 9-inch deep-dish pie shell
¹/₂ teaspoon ground ginger	

In large bowl, combine pumpkin, sugar, cinnamon, nutmeg and ginger. Add eggs. Beat lightly with rotary beater or fork just until combined. Gradually stir in evaporated milk and milk; mix well. Pour filling into pie shell on oven rack. To prevent overbrowning, cover edge of pie with foil.

Bake at 375°F for 25 minutes. Remove foil. Bake about 25 minutes longer or until knife inserted near center comes out clean. Remove pie from oven. Cool on wire rack. Refrigerate within 2 hours; cover for longer storage. Cut pie into wedges. If desired, serve with sweetened whipped cream

Nutrition information per serving (¹/₈ of recipe): calories 286; total fat 13 g; saturated fat 4 g; cholesterol 86 mg; sodium 120 mg; total carbohydrate 38 g; dietary fiber 2 g; protein 7 g

RECIPE NOTE: If desired, decorate edge of pie with baked pastry cutouts shaped like leaves and garnish plate with fresh fruit.

Pictured on pages 78–79

spice advice: garnish with seasonings

A sprinkling of Tone's ground spices, such as cinnamon or nutmeg, is an easy trim for desserts, as is a sprinkling of paprika on meats and vegetables. Tone's whole cinnamon sticks are not only easy garnishes for hot beverages, they lend their spicy flavor as well.

plum and nectarine tart

Makes 6 servings   **PREP TIME: 15 minutes**   **BAKE TIME: 30 minutes**

 2   medium nectarines, pitted, cut into $^1/_2$-inch-thick
       slices (approximately 8 ounces)
 2   large plums, pitted, cut into $^1/_2$-inch-thick slices
       (approximately 8 ounces)
$^1/_4$ to $^1/_3$ cup sugar
 2   teaspoons TONE'S Cornstarch
 2   teaspoons TONE'S Pure Vanilla Extract
$^1/_4$ teaspoon TONE'S Ground Nutmeg
       Prepared pie dough for one 9-inch pie shell
       Sugar

   In medium bowl, combine nectarines, plums, $^1/_4$ to $^1/_3$ cup sugar, cornstarch, vanilla and nutmeg, tossing to mix well. Place pie dough flat on ungreased baking sheet. Arrange fruit mixture on dough, leaving 2-inch border. Gently fold border of dough over fruit; sprinkle with sugar, as desired. Bake at 425°F for 30 minutes or until crust is golden brown. Cool slightly on wire rack. Serve warm.

Nutrition information per serving ($^1/_6$ of recipe): calories 197; total fat 7 g; saturated fat 2 g; cholesterol 0 mg; sodium 136 mg; total carbohydrate 31 g; dietary fiber 1 g; protein 3 g

RECIPE NOTE: For convenience, use prepared pie dough from the refrigerator section of the supermarket.

spice advice: stocking the cupboard

Certain herbs and spices are among the staples used in cooking and baking. Here are some seasonings to consider when stocking your kitchen cupboard: basil, bay leaves, cayenne or ground red pepper, black pepper, chili powder, ground cinnamon and ginger, dill weed, oregano, rosemary, thyme and vanilla.

Holiday Ginger Pound Cake

holiday ginger pound cake

Makes 16 servings   **PREP TIME: 15 minutes**   **BAKE TIME: 1¹/₄ hours**

³/₄ cup (1¹/₂ sticks) butter or margarine,
       softened
1¹/₂ cups sugar
   3 eggs
1¹/₂ teaspoons TONE'S Pure Vanilla Extract
   1 teaspoon freshly grated lemon peel

2¹/₄ cups all-purpose flour
   2 teaspoons TONE'S Baking Powder
1¹/₂ teaspoons ground ginger
³/₄ teaspoon salt
   1 cup plain yogurt

Using electric mixer, beat butter and sugar until light. Gradually add eggs, vanilla and lemon peel, beating until well blended.

In small bowl, combine flour, baking powder, ginger and salt; add to butter mixture, ¹/₃ at a time, alternating with yogurt and mixing until just blended. Spoon into floured greased 9 x 5-inch loaf pan.

Bake at 350°F for 1 hour and 15 minutes or until wooden pick inserted into center comes out clean. Cool in pan on wire rack 15 minutes. Remove from pan; cool completely on wire rack.

Nutrition information per serving (¹/₁₆ of recipe): calories 240; total fat 10 g; saturated fat 6 g; cholesterol 64 mg; sodium 272 mg; total carbohydrate 34 g; dietary fiber 1 g; protein 4 g

RECIPE NOTES: *To make small pound cake loaves instead of one large loaf, spoon batter into three floured greased 5³/₄ x 3¹/₄ x 2-inch loaf pans. Bake for 50 to 60 minutes. If desired, dollop slices of pound cake with whipped cream, top with berries and garnish with mint sprigs and a sprinkling of ground spice, such as cinnamon or nutmeg.*

dessert for unexpected company

Keep a pound cake on hand in the freezer to serve guests that drop by during the holidays. To freeze the cake, place the completely cooled cake on a baking sheet and freeze it just until firm. Once firm, place the cake in a freezer bag or container, seal, label with contents and date and freeze for up to 3 months. When ready to serve dessert, unwrap the cake and let it stand at room temperature for several hours to thaw.

hazelnut chiffon cake
with mocha buttercream

Makes 12 servings　　　　**PREP TIME: 20 minutes**　　　　**BAKE TIME: 1$\frac{1}{4}$ hours**

2$\frac{1}{4}$　cups cake flour
1$\frac{1}{2}$　cups sugar
　1　cup toasted skinned hazelnuts,
　　　very finely chopped
$\frac{1}{2}$　teaspoon baking soda
$\frac{1}{2}$　teaspoon salt
$\frac{2}{3}$　cup water

$\frac{1}{2}$　cup vegetable oil
　5　egg yolks
　1　tablespoon TONE'S Pure Vanilla Extract
　8　egg whites (approximately 1 cup)
1$\frac{1}{2}$　teaspoons cream of tartar
　　　Mocha Buttercream (see recipe, below)

In large bowl, combine flour, sugar, nuts, baking soda and salt. Add water, oil, egg yolks and vanilla; beat until smooth. Using electric mixer on high speed, beat egg whites and cream of tartar until stiff peaks form. Gently stir $\frac{1}{3}$ of beaten egg whites into batter; gradually fold remaining egg whites into lightened batter. Pour into ungreased 10-cup angel food cake pan. Bake at 325°F for 1$\frac{1}{4}$ hours or until top of cake springs back when touched. Remove cake from oven and immediately invert onto glass bottle or metal funnel; cool completely.

Remove cake from pan; frost top and sides of cake with Mocha Buttercream. Garnish cake with additional chopped nuts, if desired.

MOCHA BUTTERCREAM: Using electric mixer, beat $\frac{3}{4}$ cup (1$\frac{1}{2}$ sticks) butter, softened, until light. Beat in 1$\frac{1}{2}$ cups sifted powdered sugar, 2 tablespoons unsweetened cocoa powder and 1 teaspoon TONE'S Pure Vanilla Extract. Add 2 to 3 tablespoons strong brewed coffee, beating until very light and of spreading consistency.

Nutrition information per serving ($\frac{1}{12}$ of recipe): calories 516; total fat 29 g; saturated fat 10 g; cholesterol 120 mg; sodium 354 mg; total carbohydrate 58 g; dietary fiber 1 g; protein 6 g

RECIPE NOTE: To remove skins from toasted hazelnuts (also called filberts), rub nuts, while still warm, between palms of hands or in a kitchen towel. To toast nuts, see tip, page 88.

classic vanilla cheesecake

Makes 16 servings
PREP TIME: 25 minutes

BAKE TIME: 35 minutes

CHILL TIME: 3 hours or overnight

Crust
- 1   cup graham cracker crumbs (approximately 16 squares)
- 3   tablespoons sugar
- 3   tablespoons butter or margarine, melted
- $1/2$ teaspoon TONE'S Ground Cinnamon

Filling
- 2   packages (8 ounces each) cream cheese, softened
- $2/3$ cup sugar
- 2   teaspoons TONE'S Pure Vanilla Extract
- 3   eggs

Topping
- 1   cup sour cream
- 2   tablespoons sugar
- 1   teaspoon TONE'S Pure Vanilla Extract

In small bowl, combine crust ingredients; mix thoroughly. Press evenly onto bottom and up side of 9-inch springform pan; set aside.

Prepare filling. Using electric mixer, beat cream cheese, sugar and vanilla until light. Gradually add eggs, beating until blended; pour into crust. Bake at 375°F for 25 minutes or until center is almost set. Cool 15 minutes on wire rack.

In small bowl, combine topping ingredients; spread evenly over baked cheesecake. Bake at 375°F for 10 minutes. Cool completely in pan on wire rack. Cover and refrigerate at least 3 hours or overnight.

Nutrition information per serving ($1/16$ of recipe): calories 240; total fat 16 g; saturated fat 10 g; cholesterol 80 mg; sodium 181 mg; total carbohydrate 20 g; dietary fiber 0 g; protein 4 g

gingerbread gypsies

Makes 3¹/₂ dozen cookies or 2¹/₂ dozen tree ornaments
PREP TIME: 30 minutes

BAKE TIME: 10 to 13 minutes per batch

- ¹/₂ cup (1 stick) margarine, softened
- ¹/₂ cup packed dark brown sugar
- ¹/₄ cup dark molasses
- 2 cups all-purpose flour
- 1¹/₂ teaspoons ground ginger
- 1 teaspoon TONE'S Ground Cinnamon
- ¹/₂ teaspoon TONE'S Ground Nutmeg
- ¹/₂ teaspoon baking soda

- ¹/₂ teaspoon salt
- DecACake Prepared Icings for decorating (optional)
- Colored sprinkles for decorating, such as DecACake Rainbow or Silver Decors, Green Sugars, Red Sugars, Non-pareils, Rainbow Sprinkles and Cinnamon Imperials (optional)

Using electric mixer, beat margarine and sugar until light and creamy. Beat in molasses. In small bowl, combine flour, ginger, cinnamon, nutmeg, baking soda and salt; gradually add to creamed mixture, mixing until just combined. Form dough into ball. On floured surface, roll dough to ¹/₈-inch thickness. Cut out shapes.

Place on ungreased baking sheets. Bake at 350°F for 10 to 13 minutes or until lightly browned on bottom. Cool 1 minute on sheet. Transfer from baking sheet to wire racks; cool completely. Decorate as desired.

FOR TREE ORNAMENTS: Roll dough to ¹/₄-inch thickness. Cut out shapes. Bake as directed. While still soft, make a hole for hanging by carefully pushing a skewer through cookie. Decorate as desired.

Nutrition information per cookie: calories 53; total fat 2 g; saturated fat 0 g; cholesterol 0 mg; sodium 67 mg; total carbohydrate 8 g; dietary fiber 0 g; protein 1 g

RECIPE NOTE: Silver Decors (dragées) should be used only on cookies for decorations (not for consumption).

freezing cookies

Stash cookies in the freezer up to 1 month. Package them in freezer bags or freezer containers or wrap them in foil and seal. Label with the contents and date. Before serving, thaw the cookies in the container about 15 minutes. If cookies are to be frosted, wait until after they are thawed before frosting or glazing them.

Gingerbread Gypsies

cardamom biscotti

Makes 40 biscotti   **PREP TIME: 15 minutes**   **BAKE TIME: 40 minutes**

- $1/2$ cup (1 stick) butter or margarine, softened
- $3/4$ cup sugar
- 2   eggs
- 1   teaspoon TONE'S Pure Vanilla Extract
- 2   cups all-purpose flour
- $3/4$ cup chopped blanched almonds, toasted (see tip, below)
- $1^1/2$ teaspoons TONE'S Baking Powder
- $1^1/2$ teaspoons ground cardamom
- $1/4$ teaspoon salt

Using electric mixer, beat butter and sugar until light. Gradually add eggs and vanilla, beating until well blended. In small bowl, combine flour, toasted almonds, baking powder, cardamom and salt; gradually add to butter mixture, mixing until just blended.

Divide dough in half. With floured hands, shape each into 10-inch long roll. Place each roll on a greased baking sheet. Bake at 350°F for 25 minutes or until lightly browned and centers are firm. Cool on baking sheets 5 minutes.

Cut each roll diagonally into twenty $1/2$-inch-thick slices. Place, cut sides up, on baking sheets. Bake at 350°F for 12 to 15 minutes or until lightly browned, switching position of sheets halfway through baking for more even browning. Transfer from baking sheets to wire racks; cool completely.

Nutrition information per serving (1 biscotti): calories 79; total fat 4 g; saturated fat 2 g; cholesterol 17 mg; sodium 59 mg; total carbohydrate 9 g; dietary fiber 0 g; protein 2 g

toasting nuts

When your recipe calls for toasted nuts, spread the nuts in a single layer in a shallow baking pan. Toast in a 350°F oven for 5 to 10 minutes or until the nuts are a light golden brown. Watch them carefully and stir once or twice so the nuts do not burn.

chocolate cinnamon snowballs

Makes 4 dozen cookies   **PREP TIME: 10 minutes**   **BAKE TIME: 8 to 10 minutes per batch**

1 cup (2 sticks) butter, softened
1 cup powdered sugar
2 tablespoons unsweetened cocoa

1 tablespoon TONE'S Ground Cinnamon
2¼ cups all-purpose flour
     Powdered sugar

Using electric mixer, beat butter, 1 cup powdered sugar, cocoa and cinnamon until light. Gradually add flour, mixing until just blended.

Shape dough into 1-inch balls. Place 1 inch apart on greased baking sheets. Bake at 400°F for 8 to 10 minutes or until lightly browned. Transfer from baking sheets to wire racks; cool slightly. Roll in powdered sugar; cool completely on racks. Re-roll in powdered sugar.

Nutrition information per serving (1 cookie): calories 76; total fat 4 g; saturated fat 2 g; cholesterol 10 mg; sodium 39 mg; total carbohydrate 10 g; dietary fiber 0 g; protein 1 g

rich cinnamon cookies

Makes 5 dozen cookies
PREP TIME: 10 minutes   **CHILL TIME: 2 hours**   **BAKE TIME: 8 to 10 minutes per batch**

1 cup (2 sticks) butter, softened
1 cup powdered sugar

1 tablespoon TONE'S Ground Cinnamon
2¼ cups all-purpose flour

Using electric mixer, beat butter, powdered sugar and cinnamon until light. Gradually add flour, mixing until just blended. Shape dough into 8-inch long roll; wrap in plastic wrap. Refrigerate 2 hours or until firm.

Cut roll crosswise into ⅛-inch-thick slices. Place on lightly greased baking sheets. Bake at 400°F for 8 to 10 minutes or until edges just begin to brown. Transfer from baking sheets to wire racks; cool completely.

Nutrition information per serving (1 cookie): calories 52; total fat 3 g; saturated fat 2 g; cholesterol 8 mg; sodium 31 mg; total carbohydrate 6 g; dietary fiber 0 g; protein 1 g

chocolate decadence
bread pudding

Makes 6 servings   **PREP TIME: 15 minutes**   **COOK/BAKE TIME: 1 hour**

- 3 cups whole milk, divided
- 4 ounces semisweet chocolate
- ³/₄ cup sugar
- ¹/₄ cup (¹/₂ stick) butter or margarine
- 5 cups firm white bread cubes (1 inch)
- 2 teaspoons TONE'S Pure Vanilla Extract
- ³/₄ teaspoon TONE'S Ground Cinnamon
- 3 eggs, lightly beaten

Topping
- Whipped cream, chocolate shavings or curls and TONE'S Cinnamon Sticks (optional)

In large microwave-safe bowl, combine 2 cups milk, semisweet chocolate, sugar and butter. Cover and microwave on HIGH (100%) 7 to 10 minutes or until chocolate is melted, stirring once. (Microwave ovens vary; cooking times may need to be adjusted.)

Add bread cubes to chocolate mixture; stir in remaining 1 cup milk, vanilla and cinnamon. Gradually add eggs, stirring to mix well; pour into buttered 1¹/₂-quart baking dish. Bake at 350°F for 45 to 55 minutes or until knife inserted into center comes out clean. Cool slightly on wire rack before serving. Garnish with whipped cream, chocolate shavings and cinnamon sticks just before serving, if desired.

Nutrition information per serving (¹/₆ of recipe): calories 476; total fat 22 g; saturated fat 12 g; cholesterol 147 mg; sodium 342 mg; total carbohydrate 60 g; dietary fiber 4 g; protein 11 g

chocolate trims

For elegant shaved chocolate garnishes, make short, quick strokes across the surface of a chocolate bar with a vegetable peeler. To make chocolate curls, carefully draw the vegetable peeler across a chocolate bar. For wide curls, use the broad surface and for narrow curls, use the narrow side of chocolate bar.

Chocolate Decadence Bread Pudding

no-bake spiced sugarplums

Makes 4 dozen sugarplums   **PREP TIME: 25 minutes**

¹⁄₄ cup honey	2 cups finely chopped toasted almonds
2 teaspoons freshly grated orange peel	1 cup finely chopped dried apricots
1¹⁄₂ teaspoons TONE'S Ground Cinnamon	1 cup finely chopped pitted dates
¹⁄₂ teaspoon ground allspice	Powdered sugar
¹⁄₂ teaspoon TONE'S Ground Nutmeg	

In large bowl, combine honey, orange peel, cinnamon, allspice and nutmeg; mix thoroughly. Stir in almonds, apricots and dates. Shape mixture into ³⁄₄-inch balls. Sprinkle lightly with powdered sugar before serving, as desired. (They may be stored in airtight container up to 2 weeks; sprinkle with powdered sugar just before serving.)

Nutrition information per serving (1 cookie): calories 56; total fat 3 g; saturated fat 0 g; cholesterol 0 mg; sodium 1 mg; total carbohydrate 8 g; dietary fiber 1 g; protein 1 g

country spiced fruit

Makes 4 servings
PREP TIME: 15 minutes   **COOK TIME: 10 minutes**   **CHILL TIME: 3 hours or overnight**

2 cups assorted fresh fruit, such as blueberries, melon balls, grapes and sliced strawberries, peaches, nectarines, plums or pears	**Sauce**
	¹⁄₂ cup dry white wine or white grape juice
	¹⁄₃ cup sugar
	¹⁄₂ small lemon
	12 whole cloves
	1 TONE'S Cinnamon Stick

Place fruit in large heatproof bowl; set aside. In small saucepan, combine sauce ingredients; cook over medium-high heat until sauce thickens and begins to boil. Reduce heat; simmer 5 minutes, stirring occasionally. Pour over fruit; cover and refrigerate 3 hours or overnight. Discard lemon and spices; serve with cookies or over ice cream, if desired.

Nutrition information per serving (¹⁄₄ of recipe): calories 124; total fat 0 g; saturated fat 0 g; cholesterol 0 mg; sodium 3 mg; total carbohydrate 27 g; dietary fiber 1 g; protein 1 g

flavoring suggestions

Cinnamon, oregano, chili powder, basil—what herb or spice are you craving today? Here, some of the recipes in this book are categorized under a few of our most popular flavors, so you can turn to the flavors you seek.

index

Metric Cooking Hints

By making a few conversions, cooks in Australia, Canada and the United Kingdom can use these recipes with confidence. The charts on this page provide a guide for converting measurements from the U.S. customary system, which is used throughout this book, to the imperial and metric systems. There also is a conversion table for oven temperatures to accommodate the differences in oven calibrations.

Product Differences: *Most of the ingredients called for in the recipes in this book are available in English-speaking countries. However, some are known by different names. Here are some common American ingredients and their possible counterparts:*

- Sugar is granulated or castor sugar.
- Powdered sugar is icing sugar.
- All-purpose flour is plain household flour or white flour. When self-rising flour is used in place of all-purpose flour in a recipe that calls for leavening, omit the leavening agent (baking soda or baking powder) and salt.
- Light corn syrup is golden syrup.
- Cornstarch is cornflour.
- Baking soda is bicarbonate of soda.
- Vanilla is vanilla essence.
- Green, red or yellow sweet peppers are capsicums.
- Golden raisins are sultanas.

Volume and Weight: *Americans traditionally use cup measures for liquid and solid ingredients. The chart, right, shows the approximate imperial and metric equivalents. If you are accustomed to weighing solid ingredients, the following approximate equivalents will be helpful:*

- 1 cup butter, castor sugar or rice = 8 ounces = about 250 grams
- 1 cup flour = 4 ounces = about 125 grams
- 1 cup icing sugar = 5 ounces = about 150 grams

Spoon measures are used for smaller amounts of ingredients. Although the size of the tablespoon varies slightly in different countries, for practical purposes and for recipes in this book, a straight substitution is all that's necessary.

Measurements made using cups or spoons always should be level unless stated otherwise.

Equivalents: U.S. = Australia/U.K.

$1/8$ teaspoon = 0.5 ml
$1/4$ teaspoon = 1 ml
$1/2$ teaspoon = 2 ml
1 teaspoon = 5 ml
1 tablespoon = 1 tablespoon
$1/4$ cup = 2 tablespoons = 2 fluid ounces = 60 ml
$1/3$ cup = $1/4$ cup = 3 fluid ounces = 90 ml
$1/2$ cup = $1/3$ cup = 4 fluid ounces = 120 ml
$2/3$ cup = $1/2$ cup = 5 fluid ounces = 150 ml
$3/4$ cup = $2/3$ cup = 6 fluid ounces = 180 ml
1 cup = $3/4$ cup = 8 fluid ounces = 240 ml
$1 1/4$ cups = 1 cup
2 cups = 1 pint
1 quart = 1 liter
$1/2$ inch = 1.27 cm
1 inch = 2.54 cm

Baking Pan Sizes

American	Metric
8x1$1/2$-inch round baking pan	20x4-cm cake tin
9x1$1/2$-inch round baking pan	23x3.5-cm cake tin
11x7x1$1/2$-inch baking pan	28x18x4-cm baking tin
13x9x2-inch baking pan	30x20x3-cm baking tin
2-quart rectangular baking dish	30x20x3-cm baking tin
15x10x1-inch baking pan	30x25x2-cm baking tin (Swiss roll tin)
9-inch pie plate	22x4- or 23x4-cm pie plate
7- or 8-inch springform pan	18- or 20-cm springform or loose-bottom cake tin
9x5x3-inch loaf pan	23x13x7-cm or 2-pound narrow loaf tin or pâté tin
1$1/2$-quart casserole	1.5-liter casserole
2-quart casserole	2-liter casserole

Oven Temperature Equivalents

Fahrenheit Setting	Celsius Setting*	Gas Setting
300°F	150°C	Gas Mark 2 (slow)
325°F	160°C	Gas Mark 3 (moderately slow)
350°F	180°C	Gas Mark 4 (moderate)
375°F	190°C	Gas Mark 5 (moderately hot)
400°F	200°C	Gas Mark 6 (hot)
425°F	220°C	Gas Mark 7
450°F	230°C	Gas Mark 8 (very hot)
Broil		Grill

*Electric and gas ovens may be calibrated using Celsius. However, for an electric oven, increase the Celsius setting 10 to 20 degrees when cooking above 160°C. For convection or forced-air ovens (gas or electric), lower the temperature setting 10°C when cooking at all heat levels.